Issue 48 (Spring 2022)

Editor-in-Chief:	J.R. Allen
Fiction Editor:	Dan Massett
Creative Nonfiction Editor:	Kelsey Timmerman
Poetry Editor:	Hanna Litwinowicz
Art + Innovative Media Editor:	Dalanie Beach
Media Director:	Sof Voet

Issue 49 (Fall 2022)

Editor-in-Chief:	K Anand Gall
Fiction Editor:	Madison LaTurner
Creative Nonfiction Editor:	Harrison Mmerenu
Poetry Editor:	Jordan Green
Art + Innovative Media Editor:	Kate Isaacs
Media Director:	Bella Gross

Editorial Staff

Ritika Bali
Matt Farley
Harrison Mmerenu
Sean Pierson
Cody Tieman

Abigail Denton
Hallie Fogarty
Diego Nguyen
Xavier Prince
Tyayia Young

Adefemi Fagite
Sophia Judge
Chiamaka Onu-Okpara
Kendra Stiers

Oxford Magazine (OxMag) is published biannually from the MFA program at Miami University in Oxford, Ohio. Since our premiere in 1984, our magazine has received Pushcart Prizes for fiction and poetry and published authors including Charles Baxter, William Stafford, Robert Pinsky, Stephen Dixon, Helena Maria Viramontes, Andre Dubus, and Stuart Dybek.

We seek innovative fiction, poetry, new media, and creative nonfiction/essays. Visit us online at **http://miamioh.edu/oxmag** for full submission guidelines as well as further work in prose, poetry, art, and new media.

The Golden Ox is an annual contest honoring the best in flash fiction and micro creative nonfiction. We are proud to publish the winners of the 2022 contest here.

Contact us via email at oxmag@miamioh.edu.

Managing Editor: Joseph Bates

Miami University is located within the traditional homelands of the Myaamia and Shawnee people, who along with other indigenous groups ceded these lands to the United States in the first Treaty of Greenville in 1795. The Miami people, whose name our university carries, were forcibly removed from these homelands in 1846.

ISBN: 9798376717530

Cover art: Sabin Timalsena

Cover design: K Anand Gall

© 2022 Oxford Magazine

Contents

From the Editors   7

Issue 48 (Spring 2022)

Fiction

    Nanami Fetter
    Favorite Flower   87

    Kolena Jones Kayembe
    Girls   25

Creative Nonfiction

    Lucian McDowell
    Encoded   120

    Isabella Garces
    Performance and Applause   65

    Mary Elise Myers
    My Short Life as a White Trash
    Debutant   103

Poetry

    Sarah Dayley
    Late at night I remember the first
    time you kissed me your neck
    smelled like peaches   75

	LAINE DERR	
	Just Love	24
	ROBIN GOW	
	Paper Doll	76
	CASSADY O'REILLY-HAHN	
	Weather Vane	102

The 2022 Golden Ox Award

1st Place	HEIDI NIELING	
	The Hand of God	9
2nd Place	BRETT BIEBEL	
	Deli Sliced Right	71
3rd Place	MELISSA ROTERT	
	Lindy Bird Fly	116

Issue 49 (Fall 2022)

Fiction	MAX KRUGER-DULL	
	Money from the Slick Man	12
	MARINA RAMIL	
	Because of You, I Write	78
Creative Nonfiction	DALANIE BEACH	
	Tits	84
	EMILY LAKE HANSEN	
	i say this only with love	132

Poetry

LORELEI BACHT
after another's arm — 96

a recipe for disaster — 98

the house we will not build — 100

ANON BAISCH
Forgetting Sonnets — 20

EMILY BILMAN
Chalk-Hills — 74

ROHAN BUETTEL
Aeolian Geomorphology — 18

Contributors — 147

From the Editors

Issue 48 (Spring 2022): A Note from J.R. Allen

When I was younger, I was a sprinter for my school's track & field team. My favorite race was the 4x100-meter relay. It wasn't the rush of my own 100 meters that I liked, but the camaraderie of working together on one race. You have the baton, you hand it off to me, I run, I hand it off to the next runner. Working on issue 48 of *OxMag* wasn't much different, though the number of writers, readers, genre editors, and editors-in-chief who've gotten their hands on the baton since *OxMag* was founded in 1984 are far greater in number. This print anthology wonderfully captures that same camaraderie, the brief moment where one sprinter's outstretched arm places the baton into the open palm of the next. When issue 48's editorial team and I were planning the issue, we held our meetings in the magazine's office, where there are two bookshelves, one of them half-full of *OxMag* back issues from the bygone era when it was last in print. Flipping through the pages of an almost 40-year-old issue of the very same magazine we were working on filled me with a sense of literary lineage, and I'm so proud to have gotten to work with the editors and contributors for issue 48. And, as one baton gets passed onto the next runner, and the next, and so on, I hope that one day, maybe another 38 years from now, in the same office with the bookshelf full of *OxMag* back issues, the magazine's editors (or anyone lucky enough to get their hands on a copy!) can blow the dust off of this anthology and marvel at the wonderful words we had the opportunity of publishing way back in 2022.

Issue 49 (Fall 2022): A Note from K Anand Gall

Here in Ohio, in the last week of winter break, I have been doing two things: pruning fruit trees and editing this print anthology, which marks the first print edition of *OxMag* in nearly twenty years. After nearly twenty years of print publication after our premier in 1984 (apparently we move in cycles of twenty), *OxMag* went digital sometime in 2003 or 2004. The artifacts left by editorial boards that shift annually are hazy and gray like a Southwest Ohio winter sky. There is a residue of COVID in our decision to create a physical book, a craving for a world of pulp and flesh after so many years of forced digital interaction. We long to hold things in our hands. Credit for the idea of this print edition goes to our Media Director, Bella Gross, who proposed it at the first meeting of our current editorial board. Even more fitting that it would involve a collaboration between last year's editorial board and this year's, a cross-pollination of efforts. As I search for form and space in the architecture of my apple, pear, and peach trees (an art really not terribly different from editing), I can only hope my shears are conjuring some future sweet flesh. Whatever the future holds, one thing is certain: the contributors to this anthology are the stalwart stewards of literary landscapes I am thrilled to have visited, and the harvest of words you hold in your hands is delectable. Bon Appétit!

The Hand of God
Heidi Nieling

I.

Rats can tread water for three days, says the nature documentary I'm watching with my kids. My daughter is still stuck on the fact that rats are exterminated. Even after plague, after infestation, her heart is tender and horrified. The narrator moves on to the ins and outs of how rats can swim up into toilets. My mind stays on the water treading. There was a time before this fact and a time after, and in between, there must have been experiments. I picture tanks of cloudy water in a dark basement, a single folding chair, a bare bulb buzzing at the ceiling. A scientist taking notes on a clipboard: Vigorous. Determined. And then, hopeless.

Tap, tap, tap, goes the pen on the clipboard. Scratch, scratch, scratch, go the rats at the sides of the tanks. Slowing, tiring now. Is the scientist horrified or bored? Waiting and watching for the moment she must reach a gloved hand into the tank, extend a life-saving finger to a dying rat. Like the hand of God.

II.

You are between jail cells. Behind you, it's best to be quiet at all times.

Come home quietly. Quietly do the housework. Sit quietly at the dinner table, eating spam fried in Saltines. Conditional love, they call it, when there is no love if the candlesticks aren't replaced just-so after dusting the shelves. If the dishes aren't washed in the correct order (SILVERWARE LAST), if the table isn't set the right way (KNIFE ON THE RIGHT, FORK ON THE LEFT), if the ketchup is put in the wrong spot in the fridge, if the report card isn't perfect.

When you are ushered out, cool air and bird song touches your face. The handcuffs don't clamp small enough around your wrists, so he asks if you can clasp your hands to hold them there. He says he's not worried about you, it's just protocol (IT'S ALL FOR SHOW, FOR THE NEIGHBORS, FOR YOUR MOTHER). You see the outline of every leaf in the boulevard. You see an eye peeking from across the street and you smile at it. You are finally free. You look up and swear you see the hand of God reaching down to pluck you from the earth.

III.

I decide that the scientist is bored, a little annoyed she has been tasked to watch rats try not to die. She doodles on her paper. She thinks about her childhood. She thinks about lunch. She waits. *Give up already.* She wonders if anyone would find out if she pushed the little heads under, to end everyone's misery. To move on. And what is the point of all this, anyway? She imagines it would be gentle, a soft little *plink*, like a raindrop in a puddle.

IV.

Years later, your mother tries to reach out to you. She's upbeat, friendly. How did she find you? What could she want? Hesitate, then write: *Please don't contact me again.* She sends a flurry of insults, the tamest including: *You are a failure. You'll never amount to anything.* You think: *Ah. There you are.* Find the delete button. *Plink.* Like a raindrop in a puddle. Who are you? You become powerful. You start plink-plinking everything: people, places, beliefs. You drown everything around you that has been pulling at your ankles. You become buoyant. Weightless.

V.

I wonder which side I'm supposed to be on: am I for the rat or for the scientist? On TV, there is a lion eating a zebra now, and I don't tell my kids to look away.

Money from the Slick Man

Max Kruger-Dull

At the slick man's apartment, I had a fifty-dollar bill taped to my forehead. This was after the bill was safe in my hand and before the bill was folded into my mouth. The slick man—a heavyset, theatrical man; a gray-eyed septuagenarian—used double-sided tape to stick the bill to my forehead, which was after he asked me to put my phone in his pocket and before he asked for my phone's passcode. The tape smelled like soap, or the money did, and I decided to use the fifty dollars for a new doorknob after he told me to be prepared "for a fucking" and before he told me, "This is the only money you'll be getting out of me."

NOTES

1. While reflecting on this experience, it's important to know why I think of him as a slick man. He is slick because of his ability to nudge a part of me—my hip, my nose—and guide us into the ideal position for whatever

moment he wanted us to have. Usually positionings were my job.

2. Remember: I made a mistake when dealing with the slick man. I had the fifty-dollar bill safe in my hand. For that, I did harmless things. But then he behaved as if I hadn't earned the fifty. And I felt as if I hadn't earned the fifty. For the fifty I'd only done harmless things. So he asked if I wanted to *really earn* the money and, to be amenable, I said sure. I suppose what came then was harmless too.

3. I was surprised by the nimbleness of this seventy-year-old man. But he was also surprised by me. I was taller than he expected, he said, more smiley than he expected. He told me I was less talkative than the "average whore."

4. When I was young, it was cool to care about money. After that it was gauche. And now it is cool again.

5. I will buy a gold doorknob for my bedroom with the fifty dollars. The doorknob I like is square, flat, modern-looking, and sharp. For aesthetic reasons only, I appreciate doorknobs with sharp edges. My glass doorknob fell off just days before I met the slick man. For months, I'd been having sex with a loud man, three-hundred dollars a session. Volume was his main kink. He loved when I screamed and loved to scream at me. He'd make resonant noises with his flesh against mine as if he were practicing to record an album. Whenever he walked into my bedroom, he slammed the door to scare me. We

laughed like friends when the glass doorknob fell off, producing the loudest thud. Then he asked me to be scared again.

6. The slick man taped the bill to my forehead to embarrass me and then stuffed the bill into my mouth for the same purpose but I don't get embarrassed easily. Nothing could be more humiliating than the day I lost my favorite gold pencil in second grade; I wailed and made the class look for it on the floor and then in the hallway and accused the teacher of stealing my pencil because I scored poorly on a spelling test.

7. I am getting better at acting embarrassed. I can make my face turn red without cause. In general, men come to me when they want someone to blush or cry or shiver at their provocations. If a man puts his hand on my neck, I know how to tint my gaze with fear—as is my niche. The real challenge when playing scared is restraint. "Overacting kills all boners," a friend told me. Lately I've been practicing my expressions of gratitude. A presumptuous client said those will take me far.

8. Providing a service is an unappealing concept to me. When I think of my work that way, I feel part of such a strict, dull world. But I do provide a service, sometimes of great value, sometimes of negligible importance. In school, we were taught to work hard for a dollar. We were told, "Money won't come easy to you." I sometimes confuse that to mean money shouldn't come easy. Perhaps that is why I didn't leave his apartment when the

fifty was safe in my hand.

9. When he put the fifty dollars in my mouth, I knew it was the bill, not the tape, that'd smelled like soap. I held my mouth open so all the spit would dry out and the bill wouldn't get too damp. I curled my tongue back toward my throat to minimize the germs and taste. He was pleased by my discomfort. But then he fucked me on my stomach and his force made the fifty tumble out of my mouth. It rolled to somewhere on the floor I couldn't see. So I reached over the side of the bed and felt around for my money. In the stiff position he had me pinned, I could only make vague, sweeping arm movements. There was a blanket on the floor; I rifled through its folds; I shook it out. "You move too much," the slick man said, though he was moving more than I was. I slipped out of my meekness and said, "You made me lose my money." Then I slipped my meekness back on again.

10. The encounter could've been erotic for me. I enjoy most men to varying degrees and this man was strong enough and not that hairy. But too much was going on. The money. The tape. My phone in his pocket. His need for me to be whore-like. The pain in my back from a previous fuck. My resistance to seeming business-like. I never hold on to money as tightly as I need to.

11. I was a child good at finding money on the ground: in grocery aisles around Christmas, by the register at lunch, flopping down the street. I used to pass on my findings to friends, keeping little for myself. To me back

then, money was meant to dance sillily through the world. Whenever I had cash for my classmates, they'd squeal and stash it in their pockets as if I'd demand its return. Twice, I did demand its return. Once to buy a soda. And then to throw a twenty out of our zooming school bus. "Madman!" a kid yelled at me. I laughed at the twenty. But the bill slid against the window so reluctantly, like it was teaching me its worth.

12. I had tried to orient my life around interests. I took Mandarin classes after watching *Crouching Tiger, Hidden Dragon*. Around that time, I prematurely considered becoming a translator. I loved to recite Chinese tongue twisters although I often got mixed up. Yán jiū and yān jiǔ mean two different things. In the end, my ear turned out to be lacking in the perceptiveness needed to make it far with the language. But in the class I still made sweet friends.

13. Then I became interested in pleasure: my own and then others'. The friends from grade school who accepted my gifts became friends desperately interested in money after college. I never understood how they found money itself inherently compelling, but they did, or they seemed to. They sought out money as if it were a new culture. They could hold up their hands and funds would fly to them. Now, with effort, money flies to me too.

14. After the slick man came in my hair, he let me search for the fifty as long as I allowed him to record the hunt with my phone's camera. That was when he asked for the

passcode. I still don't know why he wanted my phone in the first place; perhaps just to test my deference. So I let him record me. I crouched down and combed the floor for the fifty like I needed it to patch a hole in my skin. "It's just money," he said in a cruel voice behind the camera as I crawled. I prefer all cruelness to stop right after a man ejaculates.

15. I found the bill far from where I'd dropped it. Lately, the thought of lost cash makes me sweat.

16. When I left the slick man's apartment, I still had double-sided tape stuck to my forehead. On the drive home, I played with the fifty as if it had no value. I tossed the bill at the windshield. I squeezed the bill like it could pop. The fifty made a good Q-tip for cleaning out my ears.

17. The slick man called yesterday and offered to pay for another session: fifty-one dollars this time. "Fifty-one?" I asked. "Can I say something crude?" he asked. I said, "Go right ahead." "More cash to shove in your mouth," he said. I said, "Good thinking." And he said, "Let's make it fifty-two." I might've found him enjoyable had money not been involved.

18. Remember: I still need blinds, a strong fan, fresh towels, a firm mattress, flat pillows, a fun shower curtain, more stain remover, A/C to keep men from sweating and stinking, and, in a perfect world, bright gold forks.

Aeolian Geomorphology
Rohan Beuttel

I like to study the forms of things,
especially those created by
the action of the winds. Take the barchan,
that gritty croissant whose dynamic moves
threaten roads, railways and communications
or can trap a woman of the dunes.
It migrates, grain by grain, rising up
the gentle slope of a convex arc
to the crest of a well-sorted ridge,
only to fall down the slip-face lying
at the angle of repose. The horns
of a dilemma continue,
the inexorable march of progress
engulfs anything in its path,
passing over and leaving behind.
Too many granules and they link up to form
transverse ridges which migrate on,
the drifting sands a soliton, more than just
a wave, each particle traveling.
What lies beneath the shifting surface,
hidden now, will be revealed in time.
Wherever there is sand and a constant

motive force of wind or water
there are barchans—in earthy deserts,
on Mars, underneath the sea.

Forgetting Sonnets
Anon Baisch

04

Paling after hands __ __ __ __ __
Crippled white crippled forgetting __ __
The dust is too sparse __ __ __ __ __

Leaky window __ __ __ __ __ __
Memories and residues __ __ __
Laminar opacities laminar ~~time~~

The taking flow __ __ __ __ __ __
Footfall and edge and imprint __ __ __
And puddle __ __ __ __ __ __

The skin remains __ __ __ __ __ __
Impermeable remains __ __ __
Familiar __ __ __ __ __

Echoes are anniversaries too __
And dwindle __ __ __ __ __ __

05

White blank open __ __ __ __ __ __
Counts of __ __ __ __ __ __ __ __
You cannot keep it __ __ __ __ __

warm precipitate __ __ __ __ __
will lose __ __ __ __ __ __ __ __
move against it __ __ __ __ __ __

gravity into corners __ __ __
wet winter soil __ __ __ __ __ __
more wet __ __ __ __ __ __ __

ritual stone meme __ __ __ __ __
against wanting __ __ __ __ __ __
pressure sink __ __ __ __ __ __

scrape off the lichen __ __ __ __ __
and leave __ __ __ __ __ __ __

06 – Plum(b)

The cutting of __ __ __ __ __ __
Backing – the disappearing __ __ __
The volume body __ __ __ __ __

Uniformity :: from hand of __ __
The hanging line __ __ __ __ __ __
Exacted vertical __ __ __ __

Shadow copy close __ __ __ __ __
And weighted __ __ __ __ __ __
Graphited __ __ __ __ __ __

Source signature __ __ __ __ __
Branch of __ __ __ __ __ __ __
Stone blossom on known land __ __ __ __

All of this auspicious __ __ __ __
And her ashes __ __ __ __ __

07

Down Turning __ __ __ __ __ __
Proximal branches __ __ __ __ __
Ground under shadow __ __ __ __ __

Beneath close blanket __ __ __ __ __
weak roots __ __ __ __ __ __ __
Unemergent __ __ __ __ __

Sources __ __ __ __ __ __ __
Destinations __ __ __ __ __ __
Noncontiguous cycles __ __ __

Rotted blossoms __ __ __ __ __
A mother's dust __ __ __ __ __ __
Our alterations __ __ __ __

The history of thickness is appar~~ent~~
After cutting blood water roots down __

08

Ice outlasted __ __ __ __ __ __
But what is longevity __ __ __
Thawing ashes are meaningless __ __

Dormant grass __ __ __ __ __ __ __
Brittle broken sound __ __ __ __ __
Contractions __ __ __ __ __ __ __

Cycle of bodies __ __ __ __ __
Is linear __ __ __ __ __ __
All waves have undertow __ __ __ __

Cold white layers __ __ __ __ __ __
Eyes are dust __ __ __ __ __ __ __
There is no protection __ __ __ __

on the sidewalks there are masks __ __ __
the now faces are fracture __ __ __

Just Love
Laine Derr

Fair enough, let's speak
of reality, licking the lid
of a yogurt top, black cherry,
I pull a tube from your throat,
it's easier this way – don't
eat, don't breathe, blood-stained
smile, filled with colored glass,
hungry to tap on windows
whispering why?

Just flowers left to rot. Just bones tossed on windswept floors.
Just love (candy-coated, sticky) wriggling from your throat –

If it doesn't belong,
we cry, rip it out!

Girls

Kolena Jones Kayembe

٢ / 2

She comes down from her high and tries to piece together the details. But how does one tell time in the darkness? The hours stand still without the sun as a reference. The date and time are as much of a mystery to Nour as her whereabouts.

Maybe it is Thursday, she thinks, pulling a handful of cotton around her body. There is a draught. The air feels cold because it is wet. Shivering, Nour peers around the room but faces are lost to the shadows. Covered by fingers or sections of hair the digits and strands act as shields. The few pairs of eyes that stare back look right through her. There is no warmth or emotion, only haunted gazes of the rejected. Girls who are physically present but mentally disconnected.

Nour ignores the rumbling of her stomach and pushes her back against the wall. Damp bedrock scrapes her calves. An ache throbs between her shoulder blades. When she brings her fingers to her temple they make contact with a powdered stain. The blood that has migrated down her forehead forms a crust around her left eye. Further prodding reveals sand on her scalp and sticky clumps of hair, the roots slightly damp. When her fingers move to her lips they are so dry they split on contact. The taste of iron fills her mouth—she must have been chewing the inside of her cheek again. Nour prods the sore. Mama will scold her when she finds out.

The faint echo of the call to prayer rides on the gust of air that blasts inwards when the door at the end of the room opens. A girl is thrust, unceremoniously, into the cavernous space, stumbling forward as the man behind her steps back. There is a pause as air is sucked out of the room and the groan of rusted hinges precedes the inward swing of the door. But before the metal kisses the rocky frame a faint uttering reaches Nour's ears; the last line of the Morning Prayer. An appeal to worshippers to join the congregational assembly in the afternoon. *As-salatu khairum minan naum.*

Prayer is better than sleep.

Friday, she thinks. *Dawn*. More than a day has passed.

The idea that the world, her world, is somewhere motivates Nour to say a prayer. She shifts until she is on her knees and, quietly, recites the phrases Mama taught her. And even if women are not supposed to, Nour raises her hands from her shoulders to her ears, turning her palms and pressing them against the sides of her head. In doing so she can block out the wail of the new arrival, the foam fizzing from the girl's mouth, her flopping about like a dying fish in middle of the room. Nour squeezes her eyes shut and repeats the phrases until the *slap, slap, slap* of flesh against concrete fades. If she cannot sleep this reality away then prayers will have to suffice.

#

٣ / 3

Her eyes have adjusted to the dimness in the room, enough to make out the airshafts located a few inches from the ceiling. Like the tombs of the pharaohs, the squares let in just enough air along with slices of light. Thin beams disperse throughout the chambered darkness to leave all occupants in a perpetual twilight.

No longer dazed, Nour maps out the room's dimensions and takes inventory. She is smart and her memory is good. The room is the size of two classrooms. The ceiling is high, too high for any of them to reach. Mattresses are scattered around the room and soiled sheets are piled next to the door. There are four wooden chairs, one of which is broken. At last count, there were twenty-seven girls, three women and two children.

There is only one exit.

Groups huddle at the edges, banded together in cliques. The dynamics are immediately recognizable. She must find a way to fit in because, like at school, there are good alliances and bad ones too. Nour turns to the girl nearest to her, "I am Nour," she whispers in colloquial Arabic. The pair sit in the corner, as far from the rust-covered door as possible.

The figure lies on the mattress next to the hole where everyone relieves themselves. Nour ignores the smell and inches closer, enough to see the strong curve of the girl's back and press of thighs against her chest. This girl holds her legs in place with an arm covered in ferocious and uneven bruises. *She is my age, maybe older?* Nour thinks looking at the coils of hair and rounded cheeks covered with grime. Pubescent padding fills out her hips and heavy breasts push against the too small *abaya*. Nour has watched this girl closely because, unlike the others, she seems watchful and not as scattered. More importantly, she has not been dragged out of the room since Nour arrived, which suggests this girl has important information. Things that can help her survive this place.

She reaches out and touches the body part closest to her; a crescent moon of flesh the *abaya* doesn't cover. "I am Nour," she repeats, hand lingering on the exposed hand. "I come from West Cairo."

The girl grunts and covers her face with the sheet before flipping over to face the toilet. Nour responds to the rejection by biting the inside of her cheek and wringing her hands. Since all they have is time she will try to befriend the girl again tomorrow and, if that doesn't work, the day after that.

#

٤ / 4

The opening and closing of the door is the marker: Once around dawn and again at night. This is how Nour keeps track of time. The events a part of her mental diary. Something tells her having a basic routine is one way of maintaining her sanity.

Four men arrive as the Morning Prayer ends to add new girls to the cave and subtract others. Two men stand by the door as the exchange takes place, rifles slung across their chests, tall and lean and outfitted in t-shirts, jeans, and boots with thick laces. A mix of confidence and disgust is etched all over their faces. The two in the room wear similar clothes, but are shorter and stockier, and they don't have guns. Today, they enter swinging pieces of pipe aggressively out in front of them, as if the cylinders were extensions of body parts they wished were bigger. With a hand clasped around a rusty pipe the man with the lazy eye walks around the room and shines a flashlight across clusters of bodies and drooping faces. He sees something he likes against the far wall and grabs the closest limb, hauling the body towards the door. Five girls have been lost this way. Two have returned. Three haven't come back.

Soft cries are exhaled as soon as the door closes. Bodies

shift position. Nour's hands shake as she pulls out a piece of bread hidden in the pocket of her dress. She turns to the girl on the mattress and clears her throat before reaching out to *tap, tap, tap* what might be a leg hidden underneath a sheet that used to be the colour of sunshine.

"I am Nour, she says, I am from West Cairo, Imbaba, and I have extra bread. What about you? Are you hungry?"

There is a long pause. The sheet rustles. The girl pokes out her head and focuses her almond-shaped eyes on Nour, taking in the face with a bone structure similar to her own.

"*Qarafa*," she mumbles. "I am from the City of the Dead."

The pitch of the voice is more harmonious than Nour expected. Hands shaking, she holds out the bread, the mold brushed away.

"It's Asima," the girl says, accepting the offering.

The words slip underneath a greased curtain of hair and hover momentarily between them. *Asima*. Nour lets it fall into her cupped hands and, in one swift movement, places her palms over her heart, holding onto the name as if it were a gift.

#

٥ / 5

Nour and Asima huddle together on the dirty mattress with their heads turned towards one another. They pass a plastic bottle of warm water between them, whispering between bites of food. "I don't believe you," Nour says quietly, chewing the bread until it turns to mush and sticks to the roof of her mouth.

"We are in a cave. Look around you!" Asima says, shaking her head.

"I thought we were in a house in the desert, outside the city?"

"A house with no windows? *Ekhrasy*! You are crazy, Nour. My family is poor, like yours, but even our house has windows."

Nour bites the inside of her cheek and tries not to cry. "I am not crazy; we might be in a house and someone will rescue us soon."

Asima takes a sip of water and gives the bottle to Nour, "We didn't travel that far. I remember how I got here. We are underground, in a cave. Come on! You must have heard of such places?"

A cave in the city? Nour shakes her head. Asima has gone mad.

"*Bas habibti*," Asima replies. "There are caves like this

everywhere—under buildings and bridges. In the ground where people don't look. The caves where men keep girls who they think won't be missed at home."

Nour stops chewing. *Missing? Stolen?* She thought the stories were rumors. Her father or brothers would never force a girl to live in a hole.

"It can't be true. How do you know these things?" she asks her new friend.

Asima bows her head, hair covering her face, "I've been in a cave before. Five days, and I was lucky. Others were there for months. The police found us after a *bawab* tipped them off. He saw a group of men he didn't know coming and going from abandoned apartments at the end of his street. Hidden places are getting harder to find; when one closes another opens. Men set them up in Cairo to keep and sell things they can make money from."

"Like drugs and guns?" Nour asks.

Asima narrows her eyes, "Yes, and girls as well."

#

٦ / 6

Nour asks what happens when they get dragged out of the room, but Asima does not answer. Instead, she speaks about the best way to hide or how to avoid feeling anything when everything starts to hurt. One trick Asima taught Nour is how to scramble into position at the sound of the metal lock scraping across the door. Nour packs her body against Asima's and whips the stained fabric over their bodies, curling her spine so, like twins in a womb, they become fetal. The first lesson Nour has learned about disappearing is the importance of turning inward and shrinking.

The men with the food arrive around the last call to prayer each day. Tonight, one man stands by the door while two others toss in a dozen loaves of stale bread, a bag of boiled potatoes, and bottles of water and Coca-Cola. Before leaving they push in large plastic containers of spoiled *ful* and crusted-over *koshary*. Nour and Asima wait for the lock to slide back into place before pitching forward, arms cycling, to grab provisions. Starved, they fight the other girls for whatever they can get. At first, Nour tried to be mindful because trampling another is probably *haram*. Forbidden. But she forgets about compassion in exchange for quelling the hunger.

"*Aiwa habibti*, it is us or them," says Asima when they are back on their mattress. Holding out a potato, she congratulates Nour on their haul.

#

٧ / 7

"How did you get here?" Asima asks, wanting to know if

Nour's story mirrors her own. She suspects it will since most stories are the same in here. Nour pauses and tries to sharpen her recollection before responding with the details she remembers.

"It was Wednesday," she begins, "and I was waiting for my brother, Karim, to pick me up after school because I take an extra math class twice a week. But he sent a text to tell me to catch the bus—he had football. I jingled the handful of *piasters* Mama had given me that morning and thought about calling Baba, but he works late at the factory and I didn't call Mama because it would get Karim in trouble. Instead, I walked to the bus stop even though I hate the bus. It's crowded and there are always men who try to touch you. Is it the same in your part of the city? Anyways, I missed the bus and started to walk home, making a stop to buy a Pepsi and stick of gum with the rainbow on the wrapper; I love the orange flavour. I pulled my *hijab* forward, pushed my headphones in my ears, and turned up the volume on Myam's new song. What? Don't look at me like that, Asima, she makes great music. I had just turned off the main road onto a really quiet street when someone called my name. It was Mo! I know him from school. He's older but hangs out with guys in lower grades. It was weird because I thought he lived closer to Dokki and hadn't seen him around for a while. We have talked though and he's asked me out for soda, like, ten times, but I never went because my parents would be mad if they found out.

"I stopped and waited for him to catch up so we could

walk together. We talked about movies and music. He said he liked my outfit and makeup. I was so into our conversation I lost track of time and where we were walking. It was then a van drove up and a guy jumped from the back—cute, like Amir Karaka, you know, the movie star? He said 'hi' to Mo who nudged me forward; I thought they were friends and he wanted to introduce me. His friend dropped something and I reached for it, which was when one of them hit me on the head. All I remember after that is a cloth on my face and hearing Mo tell his friend he would see him again in a month."

Nour leans back on the mattress and waits for Asima's reprimand. She knows girls from the City of the Dead have a lot of street smarts. Imbaba girls are not known for their grit. But to Nour's surprise Asima puts down her bread and whispers, "*Khalas.*" Enough. Why hear more when Nour's story is all too familiar?

"Every detail," Asima says, "sounds just about right."

#

٨ / 8

When Asima thrashes next to her Nour pulls the sheet tighter around her body. She covers her ears with her hands and thinks about the dream where her three brothers scour every inch of the city and, with Mama and Baba's help, they find her. The dream could be real because Nour is loved as much as the boys in her family. Her mother always says so—her father too. Baba even said he thinks she is smarter than his sons, which is why he works extra hard to send her to school. She can become a teacher, nurse, or even a doctor. Baba believes his only daughter is clever enough to do anything.

Nour keeps her eyes squeezed shut and hangs on to the fading images until the door opens later that day and food arrives. Memories are the only things that make her feel safe.

Asima was taken in the morning. She will return the following day.

#

٩ / 9

The men thrive on force and use drugs to keep the girls compliant. White powder is mixed into the containers containing the runny, orange slop they call *ful*, but sometimes the men are lazy and don't mix the powder enough, so it forms visible globs. Asima saw them do it the other day, which is why she slaps the beans from Nour's hand and makes her wipe the residue on the wall behind them.

"Only eat bread and potatoes," she cautions as her fingers trace the bruise blooming along her jaw. "And no soda, only water! They sometimes put drugs in the Coca-Cola too."

Nour tries to find out what happened to her friend, but Asima ignores her and whispers about the ways order is kept, like fostering divisions and pitting girls against each other. In exchange, some are given extra food, clean clothes, or little luxuries like candy and accessories. A few girls have managed to escape by using seduction. "They make special arrangements," a girl named Intisar says. Intisar is from Shubra and almost three years older than Nour. She joined them at the back of the room two days ago.

"Girls get extras if they offer their bodies and some do it because they think they'll get cut loose," Intisar explains as the trio cluster together on the mattress. It has happened before. The men know a girl won't report them if she gets out. "There is too much shame in telling someone about this place. Besides, who would believe us?"

It doesn't make sense. "What goes on? Why won't you tell me?" Nour asks, impatiently. Intisar starts to reply but stops when Asima slaps her across the face and the three go silent. Asima considers the practicalities of a special arrangement while Nour rejects the idea; she doesn't know how to seduce someone. She's only had one boyfriend and they never kissed. Nour decides she would rather die in this cave, which is why she considers getting shot. The option seems preferable than engaging in unspeakable things. *What happens when she gets out and has to live with the memories?* Nour has enough material to haunt her for a lifetime. Ordinary noises that make her jump. Familiar food that makes her stomach turn. Commonplace items that come with connotations their creators probably never envisioned. Nour has been told of four other uses for Coca-Cola bottles aside from drinking.

Who wants to remember that? she thinks, biting her lip until she draws blood.

#

١٠ / 10

The man with the movie star face moves like a desert fox and is wrapped in a cloud of cologne. His smell warns the girls of his approach. He shines his light around the cave until it comes to rest on Nour's mattress. She is curled up, nearly invisible, save for a cracked heel poking out. The man grabs her foot and pulls her into the middle of the room. He shouts for her to lift her abaya. She cowers, not wanting to show her body, but her hands tremble and lift the cotton anyhow.

Thwack! A collective gasp is heard as Nour gets her first taste of the cane. The rod cuts through the listlessness of the air before finding unblemished skin. The man yells she will get five lashes for planning to escape. Nour has Maysun to thank for the beating. The snout-nosed girl from Ezbet el-Haggana has been in the cave longer than anyone else, Asima's guess is about thirty days. Thinner than the others, Maysun has chin-length hair and a singular brow. Most of the girls think she looks like an urban rat with her beady eyes and two square teeth poking out above her bottom lip, protruding in such a way one would think there wasn't enough room for them in Maysun's crooked mouth.

Lashes rain down as Nour cries out. Her appeal goes unheard as the man swings his arm back and the cane whistles through the air. Through her tears Nour sees Intisar hold Asima back. To her left, Maysun rocks back and forth on her heels—the girl smirks while chewing her knuckles.

Much later, after food has arrived, Asima quiets Nour's whimpers by using dirty water to clean the blistering wounds. When the oozing finally stops Asima puts pieces of bread in Nour's mouth and instructs her to chew. She also shares the tricks of how to breathe through pain and leave her body entirely.

She tells Nour of all the ways a girl can survive outside herself.

#

١١ / 11

The residue of powder is everywhere: All the food, even the bread, is laced with drugs. Nour learns quickly that hunger hurts more than the crack of the cane.

#

١٢ / 12

The next day, however, she learns of things that cause more distress than hunger, like the disgrace of being dragged out of the cave by one leg or the torment of spending hours with her face pressed against cold concrete.

The imam's voice is an echo by the time Nour reaches the end of a long hallway. She watches as the man above her knocks on a nondescript grey door. When it opens Nour is thrust into a large room awash in light. This is where the men congregate. Warm and lived in, three crowd around a TV by the entrance and yell at uniformed figures racing across a green pitch. Nour is pushed past them to the back of the room where she is handed off to a fully veiled woman. The sight of the *niqab* is confusing. *What is she doing? Why is she here?* The woman sits at a table covered by bags of powder and stacks of money and smells of vinegar and myrrh. She looks Nour up and down, eyes darting within the rectangular opening of her face covering and, after a few seconds, dismisses the man standing behind Nour. Nour determines the room is in the shape of a 'ن' when the woman takes her by the arm and leads her around a corner. The sound of the television fades as they shuffle past an old gas stove and another table filled with empty containers. Around another corner, against the back wall, there is a mattress across from a plastic bright blue basin. Above, a circular metal bar is affixed to the ceiling and from it hangs a white plastic curtain covered in yellow and green flowers.

"Get rid of the filth," the woman says, instructing Nour to take off her dress and sponge herself down. "Some men have paid good money to see you and if you behave one might take you from here."

Nour turns her back and starts to breathe heavily. Panic floods her chest as she removes the cloth covering her body. She pauses, considering how far she could make it if she runs, but the woman—who seems to read her mind—slaps her wounds with a hard, unyielding object. *Not far*, Nour thinks, stepping into the basin and squatting until her thighs touch the water. Using a small, floating bar of soap, Nour splashes her face and arms. She scrubs her skin and hair until layers of dirt lift and the water turns grey. She towels off and reaches for her dress, but the woman snatches it and instead holds out a piece of gum with a red sun on the wrapper. Nour takes it and sniffs. Cherry. The one flavour she hates.

"Good girl," the woman says, her voice made rough by the fabric covering her face. She steers Nour to the mattress and says, "Wait here while I get your first visitor." Pedaling back, she raises a gloved hand and motions to someone unseen.

Following a brief moment of possibility, come all the things Nour would rather forget such as the pain of being crushed and stretched, or the savage manner in which men dive into her, the second in particular, so heavy she fights to breathe. As old as her Baba, this man is uglier, his skin is mottled and broken. By the time the third visitor arrives Nour aches so much she can't stop crying. Her tears distress the slender man who claims to have paid three hundred pounds for half an hour. He tells Nour he will go if she touches him with her hands, so she holds them out and keeps her eyes closed until he finally leaves.

When it is over she takes a breath and thinks about her friends. It was better in the cave. But a fourth man arrives and Nour learns of the kind of fear men instill when high on hash and drunk on power. This one uses his meaty palms to cover her face as a form of erasure. After he leaves Nour notices every time she reaches her hands out they return immediately to her body.

Only hours later does she understand how the rupturing of old wounds is worse than not having enough to eat. What Intisar once said makes sense—the stories about the honor behind the ritual to become a woman were nothing but lies. Having her most intimate parts cut away does not make her pure and does little to keep her safe. The procedure all the local girls do in the name of tradition do not stop a man from taking what he thinks he is owed. This last truth hurts most, which is why Nour thinks of Asima as the final man slams into her—her cheek rubbing against concrete. There, Nour practices escaping, disappearing until she is lost and feels absolutely nothing.

#

٤ ١/ 14

Asima holds Nour and the slow rock—back and forth, back and forth—lulls the latter into a fitful, sporadic sleep. It is only when the wounds start to develop a skin of their own that Nour returns. Asima's long fingers gently untangle her hair; dark strands that resemble rivers of ink.

"What do you think of when you leave?" Nour winces as Asima's fingernail scrapes a sore on her scalp.

Asima is quiet for a long time before replying. "Depends," she says, "sometimes a song I like or those sugared coffees you can get for 50 *piasters* with the pillows of milk on top. A lot of time I don't think at all."

"What about your family?"

"Them?" Asima scoffs. "Never. Sometimes I think of my little sister, but then stop because it makes me sad. How do I keep her safe from this?"

Nour closes her eyes and whispers, "I think about my family all the time."

"Well *habibti*," Asima says, unraveling a knot at the nape of Nour's neck, "we aren't all lucky to have a family like yours. My uncle gave me up for a thousand pounds the first time so I don't trust anyone. Family especially."

#

١٥ / 15

Nour and Asima share their padded refuge with Intisar and Hayat, a new arrival from Bulaq. Asima says it is safer to be bunched together, like bananas, instead of spread out across the room. The girls wear their abayas and share thin sheets between them, fabric sometimes sporting holes so big their arms and legs poke through. Asima eats a mushy potato and looks at the marks Nour has etched on the wall next to the mattress.

"That is torture," she says.

"It helps me not go crazy," Nour replies while a voice in her head screams, *Fifteen days!* She pulls her hand back sharply.

Half a month has passed. It feels like a lifetime.

#

١٨/ 18

Seven new girls are added. Five are subtracted. The children are no longer with them. There are twenty-four girls and one woman. Maysun—who disappeared for a few days—returns, wearing a pink sweater over her abaya. Her heavily bruised hand clutches a small bag of candy.

Nour ignores the newcomers while listening to Asima tell her story for Intisar and Hayat; the one where her mother sent her to buy rice and a cousin offered to drive. The girls talk and eat and, following that, huddle on the mattress and try to sleep. Nour hasn't slept for days. None of them have. Instead, she lies on her back and gazes at the ceiling. Maybe if she stares for long enough she can find fissures for them to slip through and escape this hell together.

#

١٩ / 19

Nour wakes to the sound of Asima hissing but the warning

comes too late—she is hauled towards the exit on her belly, ribs cracking as her body *thump, thump, thumps* over the threshold. On the other side of the door she curls into a ball and catches her breath. Looking up, Nour sees the man with the movie star face pushing the long metal bar into place. He instructs the other men to go ahead.

Only when the tread of boots has faded does the man look down. He smells different today, his cologne is sweet, less aggressive. Nour feels all her muscles tense as he lifts her to her feet and places his hand, gently, on her shoulder, speaking softly as they walk down the corridor. "You have another chance," he says, sucking air between his teeth. "Three nice guys have paid to see you today and if you're good, *ya gameela*, one will pay more and take you from here."

As they approach the room at the end of the hall Nour is aware of details she missed before, like the track of lights on the walls, the rumbling of engines overhead, and the faint honk, honk, honk of traffic. Nour's sudden closeness to the outside world makes her slow her step and savour the moment. She only takes leave when she is in the basin at the back of the brightly lit room.

By the time the first man arrives Nour is already long gone.

#

٢١ / 21

Prayer is better than sleep. The imam's voice echoes as Asima is taken away again. Nour bites her nails until she reaches skin because she started to use them to scratch at her face. Hayat tries to provide comfort, but she is scared like the others. At one point, Nour brings up the idea of taking the men's weapons or using the drugs against them. Intisar rolls her eyes and tells her to shut up because her plan is full of holes.

When the door opens that evening Nour's heart thuds against her chest. She keeps her head above the sheet as containers of food are pitched forward and, to everyone's surprise, Asima is pushed in after. The ensuing commotion allows Nour to rush over and put her arms around her friend's shoulders. She guides her to the back of the room while Intisar and Hayat fight for the day's meal.

Nour caresses Asima's back. Intisar rations out potatoes. Hayat washes away the blood from wounds that cause so much pain Nour tells Asima to stay away for as long as needed. She can return when the time is right but, for now, the safest place is one that cannot be accessed from the outside.

#

٢٥ / 25

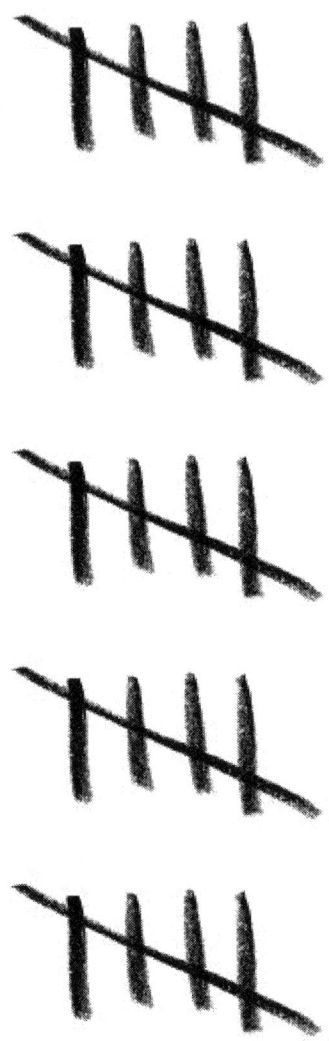

Nour completes the last line. The gash on her index finger bleeds.

#

٢٧ / 27

Nour's pain originates from behind her breastbone to spread across her chest. She feels hot and her skin is damp. The others aren't sure what is happening, but Hayat knows because her auntie is a nurse. She approaches a lanky girl across the room and trades a bottle of Coca-Cola and shiny barrette for two paracetamols. Hayat crushes the medicine and gives it to Nour before trying to bring the fever down by placing a wet sheet on Nour's forehead.

Asima is also having trouble. She is sick in a bad way. The lacerations will not close and she's been throwing up for days. She complains of a soreness all over, her breasts and abdomen in particular.

Everyone knows what Asima's problem is. Asima included.

#

٢٨ / 28

Afaf is beautiful—they see it and Afaf knows it. Her eyes

are bright and her hair gleams as if slathered with almond oil. She's a flash of colour in this cavernous gloaming. A flower in a desert oasis, Afaf has an innocence the rest lack. Her purity makes the other girls bristle.

Maysun shouts at the new arrival from her pile of fabric, saying things that would make any mother wash her mouth out with soap. But while everyone hates Maysun because she is cruel, no one says a word because they hate Afaf more. Everyone is envious of the most beautiful girl in the room.

Afaf shuffles to the other side of the makeshift toilet where she begins a slow wilt until she hits the floor. Nour rocks on her tailbone and thinks about offering Afaf the piece of hardened bread tucked under the mattress, but as she reaches for it Asima's fingers wrap around her upper arm.

"No," she says. "You don't want to mess with that."

Why not? Nour slumps against the wall. "Look at her," Nour says. "She is like us! Look at her weep."

Afaf's hands hide her face as a stream of tears slip through her delicate fingers, glistening in the darkness. Even her distress is beautiful. Nour feels the return of her heart's ache.

"You can't help her," Asima looks down. "She'll be gone by tomorrow. Beauty like that always fetches a good price."

Nour's bottom lip trembles as Asima squeezes her arm. "I know," she says, "isn't it sad when even beauty cannot save you? Nothing stays pure in a place like this."

#

٣٠ / 30

Afaf is taken and another girl is thrown into the room. This one has sallow skin, cropped brown hair, and rings of kohl smeared around pale eyes. She is rabid. Undomesticated. Her febrile yelps echo as she stares groggily at the roof. Feral, this girl has the look of one who has lived underground for too long.

Nour takes a step but is intercepted by Maysun who scuttles across the room to grab a fistful of Nour's hair. "What are you doing?" she hisses. The breath hitting Nour's face is rancid like soured milk.

"*Keda kifaya!* Enough! I'm helping because she's hurt."

"Of course she's hurt. She's *sharmota!*" Maysun is so close Nour can see the throbbing cyst on her chin. Nour has the sudden urge to reach out and shake Maysun until her brains come loose. They are all whores down here.

"Leave me," Nour says as she kneels next to the young woman.

"So foolish!" Maysun seethes. "Always trying to help. Desperate to be liked. *Behiima*! How have you not figured out, Imbaba girl, we are probably a few blocks from your home? Why haven't your friends told you how close your family are?"

There is a stirring behind them. Asima growls. Intisar shouts. Nour stands and turns her head towards Maysun.

"What did you say?" she asks.

"You heard me, *bint-el sharmota*," Maysun laughs. "Our cave is in Imbaba."

"*Tozza feek, kaddaab!*" Asima shouts as she hurls herself across the room. She swings her arms and tells Maysun to screw herself, her bitterness is poisoning them all. While Asima delivers enough blows to take the breath from Maysun's mouth, pieces of the puzzle fall into place for Nour. Pressing her body to the wall, she propels the back of her head against exposed rock trying to jangle the words from between her ears. Done with Maysun, Asima pulls Nour towards their mattress and tries to calm her with no luck. It is only when the sheet flutters over their bodies that Nour issues a howl the others feel ricocheting deep within their chests.

#

٣١ / 31

"I am close to home? The cave is in Imbaba?" Nour's

muttering is so constant it turns into an invocation. A poor girl's chant.

"Yes," Asima says, cradling Nour's head. She has held onto the delicate dome for a day, trying to push a few breadcrumbs past her friend's broken lips.

I am close to home? I am close to home. "You knew," Nour says.

Asima looks at the ceiling and nods. She opens and closes her mouth.

"Why didn't you tell me?"

"What for? So you could beat your head against the wall until you die?"

"I trusted you," Nour says. "You could have told me."

Asima shrugs, "I did what I thought was best. We are looking out for you."

"Shut up," Nour sniffles, turning her back on Asima. She stares at the wall and bites the inside of her cheek until pieces break free. Only when the taste of blood becomes too much does Nour close her eyes. She does not sleep.

#

Nour hasn't eaten for days. Asima and the others pile food and water in front of her, waiting for their Imbaba girl to snap out of her stupor. Asima offers her half of the sheet to Nour, but absolution will take time now that she has fled to the deepest parts of her mind. Physically present but mentally absent, Nour is not in the cave. She is at the *Iftar* table where the members of her family are seated. They crowd around bowls of food. Her brother laughs. An uncle prays. They load up their plates and break the fast. Together, Nour and her family put their hunger to rest.

The feeling of Asima's arm jars her awake. Nour tries to twist away but Asima holds on. The two struggle until Nour gives up. Exhausted, she collapses against her friend's bony frame, wanting to cry but there is nothing left. Nour is all dried up.

#

٣٣ / 33

The day is spent praying, reaching for something good. Nour starts by telling God she is grateful for Asima. She loves her the way she would a saviour, blindly and with desperation. She loves Asima despite hating her for the lies. Deep down, Nour suspects many things can be forgiven. Her friend tried to protect her, even if she failed. The attempt alone makes Nour think they will, together, weather this storm—the first of many since life is nothing but a litany of squalls and bad weather.

#

٣٤ / 34

The door opens before the evening prayer, causing a frantic rush of bodies around the room. Girls seek cover wherever they can. Two men head straight for the mattress next to the toilet. A beam of light passes over blanketed bodies. "Where is Asima?" The man with the lazy eye shouts, trying to sound mean. "She needs to come with us. We will hurt her if she resists."

Under the sheet Asima's breath is warm on Nour's face. She holds her friend's hand and squeezes. "I have a plan, please trust me." These are Asima's last words to Nour before she lets go and slithers from underneath the cover. The man with the lazy eye reaches for her, but Asima slaps him away. She stands and pats down the front of her rags.

"*Ma'a nafsee*. Lead the way," she gestures towards the door.

Two of the men are so surprised by the insubordination they wait, but the third surges forward, grabbing Asima by the hair and yanking her towards the exit. Eyes widen as their protector stumbles through the doorway and into the dimly lit hallway. The collective breath is released when the hinges squeak, the door closing with a soft thud.

\#

٣٥ / 35

Nour looks at the imprint Asima left behind on the mattress and turns to the wall to add another line.

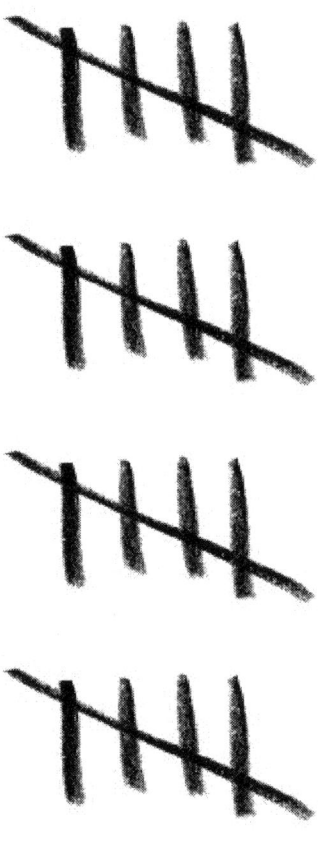

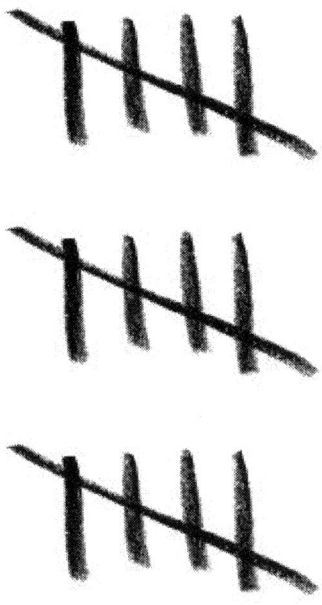

An old cut on her finger opens again. The pain feels good.

#

٣٧ / 37

Movie Star Man is the first to enter. His jeans are ripped at the knees and red t-shirt has DON'T PANIC scrawled across the front. The scowl on his face eclipses his handsomeness, making him look ugly. A dressing of metal on his knuckles glints in the subterranean twilight.

Maysun doesn't respond when called for, but he finds her and pulls her into the middle of the room. There, Movie Star Man beats her so hard one eye swells shut and a tooth flies out of her mouth. When she stops moving he takes a cloth from the pocket of his jeans and wipes his hand. Before heading for the door he spins on his heel to deliver a final kick to the ribs. On his way out, he tells the other men to clean up his mess. The shorter of the two closes his mouth and backs towards the exit while the taller one goes over to Maysun and takes ahold of her limp arms. The door closes behind them.

It is the last the girls will see of their cave rat and Nour knows compassion is the appropriate response for such a brutal departure. But she is momentarily confused when she feels relief spread across her chest. With her nails digging into her temples and lips stretched into a smile she looks around the room to see the grin mirrored back. At that point Nour stops reaching for compassion. Clearly, Maysun won't be missed.

#

٣٩ / 39

Nour resigns herself to the following: She is no one. A (no)body. She is an every-other-girl from one of Cairo's poorest neighbourhoods and will be stuck underground until some man pays the right price or she finds a way out.

Every day she prays for death and every day those prayers go unanswered. She feigns a smile in the other room, washing her arms and whispering the lyrics of the Myam song she loves. Nour does her best to be good, but it isn't enough. The traitor woman rushes over after the last man leaves.

"Stupid girl! They paid half because you cried!" The woman's shouts grow louder with every slap that connects with Nour's face.

Nour returns to the cave the same day, ashamed for multiple reasons. But the main one being she is horrible at pretending. Of little value to anyone, Nour finally gets it—she isn't worth a thing.

#

٤٢ / 42

Hayat goes limp when she is dragged through the door. Intisar tells Nour someone in Hayat's family gave her up for fifteen hundred pounds. If she is bought to be a bride the people who run the cave will earn six times that much for a girl her age.

By the time the food comes Intisar has broken the skin of her wrist with a splintered piece of broken chair. Nour wrestles the wood from her, tossing it down the toilet hole and wrapping Intisar's superficial slashes with strips of cloth. She then turns her attention to the food she managed to secure, giving a bit of everything to Intisar before eating as much beans as her stomach can hold. The white powder is visible but she stuffs the mess in her mouth anyhow. It is time to vanish as quickly as possible from this good-for-nothing place.

#

٤٤ / 44

It might be evening. The girls can't be sure. They haven't heard the call to prayer. None of the men have come since the day Hayat was taken. No longer fearful of a beating, Intisar bangs her fists on the door and yells until she loses her voice. A few others stand beside her and do the same. The sudden absence of the men has made everyone uncomfortable. They were used to the routine. Hungry for food and desperate for water, some shake in the corner while others have already passed out. Of all the ways to leave this cave Nour never contemplated she would starve. *What a horrible way to die.* She gets up and walks over to the exit and stands next to Intisar, slamming the metal with the palm of her hand until her skin turns red and bones start to ache. Only when her arms tire does Nour let out a scream that originates from deep in her belly. Bereft and arcane, it goes on, and on, and on until she runs out of breath and turns to find everyone staring—eyes full of fear at what has been unleashed. Nour lowers her hands and shuffles over to her corner to brush off a potato hidden in the mattress. She holds out half to Intisar and chews on the rest.

#

٤٥ / 45

Tap, tap, tap, is the sound. It is followed by the patter of feet and slow scrape of metal. The door opens and beams of light flicker around the room. Matronly murmurings are heard as a cluster of women in long dresses enter the cave and disperse. There are five, ten, or maybe more. The women whisper urgently to each other as they fan out. There is agency in their voices.

"What is your name?" The woman approaching the corner has an accent that is warm and familiar. She reaches out to the two bodies on a dirty mattress. "I am Marwa," she says. Nour pokes her head out from under the sheet. The room is filled with so much light she thinks has died. Maybe she is on her way to heaven right now.

"Heaven?" Marwa chuckles sadly. "No, you're alive. We have flashlights because we had no idea how many of you we would find."

Marwa helps the girls sit upright and places clean blankets over their shoulders. She brushes the hair from Intisar's face and asks, "Are you Nour?" Intisar shakes her head and points. "That is Nour," she mumbles. Another woman rushes over to Intisar while Marwa reaches for Nour. Womanly flesh wraps and embraces an adolescent body. Nour flinches as Marwa uses her weight to pull Nour up and guide her towards the door. "I am from Imbaba, like you," Marwa says as she takes Nour to the end of the long hallway where a large black door is propped open. "You are safe," she whispers, helping Nour over another threshold.

They step outside and sunlight bounces off everything into Nour's eyes. She squints and looks around, noticing the wall of concrete running over their heads. The blast of horns is deafening. Black puffs of exhaust float horizontally in the sky before turning grey and merging with cloud cover. Policemen in white uniforms race between a patrol van and ambulance. Two women with bejeweled abayas enter the cave holding a stretcher between them. A young doctor leans over a girl and examines the gash on her face. When Nour looks at Marwa she notices the hijab she wears has the same trim as her mother's.

"I work at a place that…" Marwa stops to help Nour into the large passenger van idling under the overpass, "well, we follow tips and, thankfully, it did not take long to find you."

Nour tries to unclench her fists as Marwa uses a wet cloth to wipe the grime from her face. "I know you are tired and hungry, and—" the older woman's voice falters, "but we have to take you to the station so you can tell us what happened. Don't worry though, I won't leave you. We are here to keep you safe."

Help? Worried? Nour looks out the window and digs her nails into her palms. She has experienced everything. There is nothing left to fear.

Marwa explains that after the station they will be taken somewhere to rest. "You will stay with us, *ya gameela*, until we reach your Mama and Baba. I have a list of parents who look for their girls and yours might be on it."

Tears begin to stream down Nour's face. She hasn't thought about her parents, brothers, or friends for ages. "Asima," she whispers. Nour wonders about the girl who is probably lost to her forever.

"Asima?" Marwa pats Nour's hand. "*Ya gameela*, she waits for you with clothes and a toothbrush. She came to our office after escaping from the man who bought her. Asima told us exactly where we could find you."

It seems impossible but Nour's mood shifts slightly. She leans her head against the window and tears skirt the corners of her mouth, bitter. She wipes them away while watching the abundance of grace women in motion have. When she tries to bite the inside of her cheek she stops before teeth cut flesh. Instead, she pictures Asima on the outside. *Are we ruined? How will we live? Who will love us?* The questions disperse when Intisar takes Nour's hand and whispers something only she can hear. The two lean their heads towards each other as the wheels of the van turn. Nour clasps her hand's friend tightly to stop the shockwaves of remembrance from returning. Intisar puts an arm around the younger girl and holds on since both their lives depend on it.

When they pull up to the station Asima stands on the front steps with others. Weeping parents. Weeping sisters. Brothers who weep currents of rage from behind their eyes.

Nour follows Intisar and thinks they might find a way to reassemble the pieces. Everything looks different in the light. Brighter. Softer. Asima wears skinny jeans, a long-sleeved shirt, and orange hijab with white spirals. She looks like a girl Nour once knew. Shifting her weight from one foot to the other, Asima smiles nervously at the girls climbing the stairs to the station. In her hand, she clutches a denim bag filled with soap, trinkets, and clothes in just the right sizes.

Intisar is the first to hug Asima. Arms wrap around bodies as whispers turn into cries. Nour gives them space, wiping her tears while pressing her arms against her chest. She is about to take a seat on the stairs, tired, when she feels a familiar touch on her shoulder. "I don't make promises I can't keep," Asima says, reaching for Nour and pulling her into their embrace.

Performance and Applause
Isabella Garces

We only went to the gymnasium because we'd heard they were giving out free cookies. We signed up for beginner classes, the ones where you do backward rolls and try to climb on the beam without getting a heart attack. We wore all kinds of leotards: sparkly snakeskin aquamarine, velvet numbers that darkened whenever you brushed your hands against the fabric, tie-dye unitards evoking Care Bears that had vomited their own Milky Way. My sister and I went once a week, frolicking like kids in a playground with uneven bars and a floor that felt like a springboard. Every day we'd look at the back wall that featured an arc composed of stars: it started with red and yellow stars, later blue, purple, eventually gold. Each star symbolized a level, ranging from Beginning and Intermediate to Advanced. I went from red to gold in one day.

The only reason I was asked to be part of the national team was because I did a back handspring in front of the coach. My stepfather had gotten a trampoline and I'd spent most days trying to arch my back until I could finally jump from my feet to my hands, coiling like a spring. I didn't know what I was doing, only that it felt good to want to do something impossible and to realize that impossible wasn't really a thing. Just like checkered Vans, Pacsun belts, and bedazzled phones probably weren't a thing outside of suburban Florida. In the greater scheme of life, though, 'impossible' was a thing, a universal concept. Except that our minds aren't universal — and our minds are the ones that define what's possible and what isn't.

My teammate's father used to joke that watching us train was like watching the marines. Our coach scared the shit out of us, and we conditioned for one to two hours a day before training, climbing two-story ropes with our legs posed at straight 90-degree angles so we'd only rely on our upper body strength. My middle school PE teacher grew to love me because I always won the quarterly physicals that tested strength, endurance, and flexibility: I could wrap my forearms around my feet, do more than ten pull-ups, and I was relatively decent at running the half mile around the quad.

There was only one boy who always managed to beat me and my pulse would always race whenever he deigned himself to talk to me. That's when I started to invite people to touch my stomach. I'd have them rub their fingers below my ribs, right above my belly button, caressing the contours of muscle below my skin. Everyone was amazed. Everyone except him. Those aren't abs, he said. Those are your ribs. You're just skinny. I told him he was wrong. I lifted up my shirt so he could see the shadows etched onto the disfigured squares marking my stomach.

Whenever I looked at myself in the mirror I thought I would have been much better looking as a boy. My flexed biceps contoured against my shoulders, my chest was flat either because I had yet to get my period or because I didn't possess genes that would eventually amount to full breasts. My hair was always gelled back until it crisped against my scalp, painful and unyielding whenever I dared run my fingers through it. The only good thing about waddling in a pre-pubescent limbo was that I never had to worry about waxing or shaving the slivers of thigh visible around my leotard.

Every day before practice, I'd conjure up a sickness or will myself to get a headache. The one day my mom didn't let me stay home with a self-imposed stomach ache, I ended up winning a leotard because I managed to swing up into a handstand on the parallel bars. But then I was back to waiting in line for my turn at the vault or trying out a glide kip mount on the bars. The twins in level five would share an inside joke, whispering to each other with their translucent, freckled skin and tooth-pick thighs. Serena, probably the most flexible of us all, would discuss an upcoming birthday party with Bianca, whose tan skin and brown eyes I'd always found the kindest of them all. Maya would quip a snarky yet witty comment, casually placing her weight on one leg as the others laughed. I'd usually sing to myself, pausing every once in a while to ask my teammates a question here and there.

I'd later equate gymnastics with the faint anxiety that would one day upend me in dinner parties. The desire to make conversation even though it wasn't offered. The political correctness of laughing even though everything said scores severely low on your scale of competent humor. A sensitivity to others' perceptions of your social sobriety and the belief that they can sense your discomfort and unsexy solitude akin to that of sitting alone in a cafeteria. The necessity to do something with your hands, look down at your phone or at the menu, sip from a coffee cup or a wine glass to give the illusion that in the midst of your silence, you possess an inkling of purpose.

I was a brick, stiff and unbending, training myself slowly to widen my legs past the screams of my ligaments. Our coach would berate us whenever we stretched. Square your hips, she'd say. You're not cheerleaders. Some people are born flexible, placidly sitting on their cervix as their legs splay in opposite directions. I had to work for it. And even then, the results were seventy degrees from the desired amplitude. Serena's back was so flexible that whenever we sat on the floor she'd arc her back until her toes swept above her head and grazed her lower lip. I dreamed about what my split jumps would look like if my limbs were more malleable, how my back walk-over would feel if my legs weren't tethered to one another.

We'd point our toes, tighten our tushies, dismount into clean landings more often than not. Our couch would ask me what my summer plans were and sigh whenever I told her I was visiting my family in South America. Those were three months I could be spending in summer camp, training four hours a day and learning the stunts necessary to pass to the next level. I would complain to my mom because our summer vacations were the reason I'd barely make it to the next level the upcoming year. In the battle between going to practice every day and going practice every day while still repeating the same level, there was a distinctively lesser evil.

Despite training me to develop burgeoning muscles and bottomless strength, gymnastics was a constant reminder of how powerless I really was. It consisted of five days a week, three hours each day, Saturday mornings and Summer months that were not mine to begin with. It was all-consuming, an inescapable reality that became a part of my every day, like church on Sundays or our yearly trip to visit my stepfather's family in Texas. Gymnastics was the dinner party with the relatives I couldn't stand, the wait at the bank teller I would have rather avoided, the various instances in life where I would have much rather preferred to stay home. When you're a kid, you can't leave when you grow bored, you can't hail a taxi simply because you don't want to spend the next hour helping your mother choose tea tree oil or the perfect ceramic dishware. You're forced to stay because unlike certain mammals that forage and hunt a few weeks after they're born, human children are incredibly helpless.

My mother didn't let me quit. Gymnastics was akin to guided tours, all-inclusive vacations, any type of field trip and outing that I would evade later on in life. Anything that has been severely planned to the point of designating food choices, allocations, pit stops, bathroom breaks, or dictating the window of time I can or cannot dedicate to any one thing, stripping me of sovereignty, regressing to a childhood impotence where I'm bereft of decision-making. A sweeping, suffocating ineptitude.

There was always a heaviness in my chest: metal clinking like Christmas, jostling like horse-drawn carriages and weighing me down like wine on an empty stomach. I'd grow to expect it, the Pavlonian response that associated breakfast with mornings, Sundays with church, summers with South America. I stood on the highest podium, my hair gelled to my skull and my legs dried with chalk. I raised both hands straight above my head, arching my arms behind me. I imagined a string tying my shoulder blades together, rubbing bone against bone. I smiled a beaming, toothy smile that stretched like the medals hanging around my neck, bathing in the inevitable correlation, cause-and-effect, or tropism that was performance and applause.

Deli Sliced Right
Brett Biebel

My girlfriend slept with this guy who worked at the Rainbow Foods up Snelling, and we waited for him in the parking lot. Me and Lyle. He talked me into it. I said, "Shit, I stepped out on her two or three times already, so I figure it's only fair, ain't it," but he said something about honor. The olden days. Barfights and switchblades, and they tell you the rules are changing, the ones about men and women and sex and desire, but maybe they're not, he said. Maybe they shouldn't be, and so there we were waiting. I didn't know what we were planning exactly, but maybe just scare the guy. Get a good look at him. Anyway, he comes out, and he's 6'5". Looks like a linebacker. He's carrying about four plastic bags all stuffed with shaved turkey and honey ham and the rest of the cheap shit, and we run up to him, and Lyle goes, "Hey, you know Rachel, don't you?"

"Who's asking?" the guy says, his voice all hoarse from something. A cold, maybe. Or else from talking over the machines.

"This here's her boyfriend," says Lyle, and he looks at me expectant. You gotta remember this is broad daylight now. 3, 4 o'clock on a Friday, and the lot's starting to fill up, and people are coming in with their kids, and everything's got that end of the day stress hanging on it, and I don't really know what to do, so I wave. I actually fucking wave.

"Hey," says the guy.

"Hey."

"Jesus Christ," says Lyle.

"You know, the thing with Rachel, I don't know if she told you, but we go back. Her brother and me, we used to play ball together, and I think it was one of those old-time nostalgia things, and it's none of my business, but she didn't tell me nothing, man. I swear. Not a goddamn word."

"You got anything good there?" I say, "Some of that Boar's Head, maybe?" I'm smelling sodium, and I haven't eaten lunch, and this whole thing was Lyle's idea anyway.

"In back," he says. "Let me. You know what, man, hold on. Wait here. Peace offering." He bolts back inside, and we hear the auto doors, and Lyle and me sit on the curb.

"And one of them little whiskey bottles too." Lyle yells, but the guy's already long gone. We don't have any cigarettes, so we just tap our feet and watch moms with too much makeup and people struggling to get on them motorized scooters and these high school kids all dressed like burnouts, and the guy's not coming back. We know this. Or, at least, Lyle thinks he does, and you can tell he's wanting to hit me, or to hit someone anyway, given we made the trip and all, and he says, "You know there's two of us, don't you? And one of him?"

"What about it?"

"Two is more than one, numbnuts, fucking think about it, and do you even love her?"

"Aw, Christ, do you?" and Lyle looks stunned by this. Hurt even.

"Fuck you," he says.

We're deadbeat silent for God knows how long after that, and I'm thinking about this scar Rachel's got underneath her shoulder, and she says it's from a firecracker, Fourth of July 1996, and it looks a little like a star. An explosion out deep in space.

"Whatever. Let's get out of this shithole," Lyle says finally, and, as he does, we see the guy exiting way down by the pharmacy. The whole other end of the store. Lyle is livid. "Pussy," he screams, dragging it out at the top of his lungs, and you can see the guy stop. The whole goddamn parking lot. Everything is in freeze time, and the guy launches one of them deli bags, and we watch it flying. Everyone watches it. It arcs across the lot and over fast-food wrappers and pop bottles and carts and rusted SUVs clocking 100, 200K, and it looks like roast beef. Pink flapping inside plastic, and in an instant I know me and Lyle are both after it. We're salivating. Our heads are going to collide mid-air, and we'll be hopelessly tangled, and, when we hit the pavement, rocks and broken glass will stick in our skins and scratch up our legs, and we'll be two dogs, really. Tearing into scraps we maybe don't even want.

Chalk-Hills
Emily Bilman

The silk-chalk in the new-born bay feels
like soft talcum powder under our steps.

Like the wind-swirled primeval sea-sands
under the mutinous seas, the grated chalk

powder now filling our hands is inodorous
yet heals the open wound in your hand.

High waves gnaw the chalk-hills, shape
them into convex moons. Wind-gusts

sweep the seas as in creation day, sculpting
the limestone layers into sheer geometries

like the transient dust that shaped our forms
from minerals, oxygen, iron, and carbon.

Late at night I remember the first time you kissed me your neck smelled like peaches
Sarah Dayley

Here inside our sleep-heavy bodies' folded pile of slumber,
   something like a spider bite in the crook of a rib:
I'm wide-eyed in the dark. The spark of fondness blinks out
and goes. Like you, it's not gentle: It's something like an itch, dragging
itself across the length of my sternum. It roils like a hedge
gone wild and raggedy, tearing up its dirt, tangling itself
in the backyard as you sleep. There's a cat yowling all night
outside this bedroom, full to the gills with your smell.

The black hole of the question unwinds itself, hungrily, in the soft
cups of my ears, scratching: Is this all? It growls. Is this it?

You are snoring and meanwhile my tiny star of love swallows
itself, ravenous, teeth gnashing, down into nothing.

Paper Doll
Robin Gow

give me the cut / out / garment /
in a 2-D / chapel / thinner /
than thin / I win / whimsy /
by bartering / width / my chin
straight / forward / girls gone /
shoulder / to shoulder / bare
for years / dreaming / girth
pursing my / lips / printing
purses like / stamps / sell me
as the whole / set / collection /
corkscrew / briefcase / hours spent
on a train / plane / trolley /
mothering till flat / leavened / or lead
we lay / stacked / deck of cards /
joker / joker / joker / turn a page /
and the self / spun / blank /
a glimpse of air / could undo / me
cutting along / line / linkage
to marbled / journal / pressing
necklace / to thumb / I held
my breath to keep / my clothes on /

what I wouldn't give / to print /
another / form / figure

Because of You, I Write
Marina Ramil

They say dark painted walls make a room look smaller but these, the color of blackberry juice, contain multitudes. There's a dog in the corner snoring, a hound resting his jowly face and heavy ears on wide, wrinkled paws. I stand by the wooden table with unfinished edges, two slabs joined together by butterfly joints. Someone laid a sheet of periwinkle muslin across it and dotted it with their dishes. A stew still so hot it's bubbling, the chunks of carrot and potato bobbing up to the surface then sinking out of sight. An intricately woven loaf of bread someone has lovingly strewn sprigs of rosemary atop. A pot of rice that had been tipped over onto a platter so you could see the crisped bottom, golden and glistening with oil. A bed of greens torn by hand then tossed in vinaigrette and topped with walnuts and dried cranberries. A quaint blackberry pie with a ceramic dove bursting forth from its center. A large crystal bowl of steaming wassail dotted with orange slices. Even at the edges of the room farthest from the heat of the food, this party was uncomfortably warm. People were standing too close to one another. Pink scarves were draped over lamps so they'd cast tinted light. The hum from the stereo was familiar modal jazz.

A tall red fox stood in a tweed three-piece suit.

I wasn't watching when he came in but recognized immediately that the sage green scarf hung on the coat rack by the door was his. Tight double crochet. Someone made that scarf for him. They used their own two hands. They bent over the yarn for an hour or two. They held it up every once in a while to see if it was long enough, good enough for him yet. And he had taken it off and hung it on the coat rack.

He did not talk to anyone on his way over to me. He did not look at them. He looked at me, looked down his long, straight snout at me.

When I was four feet tall, I would let the screen door slam shut behind me while my mother chopped onions for dinner. We had a great big fence of rotting wood and grass too tall. On a more stable picket, a tendril of green garden peas grew. I would pick as many as I could fit in my sweaty palms and wait for it. When it came, a bag of bones and red fur with a tail like a switch flicking behind it, I would turn to make sure my mother wasn't looking and stick my hands out at it. It ate the pea pods one by one off my hands. Once, it caught my skin with a tooth and stared at me with big brown eyes, ashamed, before running off. I'd tell my mother I had given myself a paper cut from turning the pages too quickly on my big, beautiful animal encyclopedia. I'd bandage it myself and she'd give me a sippy cup of juice. She didn't bother to check for herself what it looked like and I would go back to the fox the next night, pretending like what happened hadn't happened.

This fox, the one standing on two feet in oxfords, lifted a paw to tuck a strand of hair behind my ear and sighed, "I'm probably going to head out. I can't do the whole potluck thing. I want to be able to sit down and take my time, y'know? And I hate talking to these people, y'know?"

He looked off at the crowd around us and I thought I did know but wished I didn't.

"Okay. I said I was going to go back to hers soon anyway for that other thing."

That night the fox of my childhood bit me, I sat up in my twin bed and prayed for five minutes more than I usually would. I prayed for everything I knew just in case. I prayed for the fox. That he'd get more food. That he'd find a good home. That the cut on my hand would heal well. That when the scab became a scar and I kept growing someday I would barely see it. That no one would ask where it had come from. That he'd come back tomorrow even if he bit me again. That he'd keep coming back even if he bit me every single time.

When I told the fox, the one wearing the kind of jacket with patches on the elbows, that I would be leaving too, just as he had told me he planned to a moment before, he breathed out a little laugh.

"What?" I said it as quietly as I could, so maybe he wouldn't hear and I wouldn't have to find out.

"I just think it's really fucked up. How often does this sort of thing happen and you're just, what? Making other plans at the same time?"

I went to school the day after the bite and told anyone who asked that it was a paper cut. Some of the other children were talking on the playground about their pet dogs. A German shepherd that lives outside and really isn't allowed inside ever. A pitbull, but we have to say he's a mix because of that law – have you heard about it? A black lab with a graying face who sometimes plops down on the ground so hard we're worried he won't be able to pick himself back up. So, I told them I had a fox. My fox was faster and stronger than their dogs. No, it's not, they would argue, because my dog runs around Kennedy Park on the weekends or totally once lifted the couch up by itself or can carry me on its back for actually a really long time even though he's pretty old. Come over to my house and see, they'd say. I would go over to their houses and see their dogs. They were just dogs. Then they would come over to my house, but the fox was never there. They'd have to take my word for it.

I can't look this fox, the one wearing a plain, gold wedding band on his finger, in the eye, but it doesn't matter. I do not put up a fight.

"Okay, so then I won't. No, you're totally right. I should have thought like… I can go over to hers for that thing any time. Whatever you were originally thinking."

He made the noise again. A little laugh that isn't a laugh that says, "You are fucking up. I am smarter than you. I still love you but I do not like you right now. However, I will never love you and protect you the same way I love and protect myself, but explain to me why I should when you are fucking up like you are right now."

The first time they put me in the booth, I begged forgiveness for lying about the source of the cut on my hand. The man on the other side of the lattice window stared straight ahead as he listened, giving no indication of his thoughts. I stared at his hands clasped in his lap, large but unmarred by calluses. The assumption, I take it, is that you will find your closure in the absolution. The act of contrition got caught in my throat. I exited the booth to perform penance with a locked jaw. The next time I saw the man it was on the school side, the sisters' dominion. He had come to see how the winter fundraiser, dollar hot cocoa for the victims of one of the disasters, was progressing. He approached me with recognition, knew my name, and asked if I wanted one of the steaming styrofoam cups. I said I didn't have the money and he knelt down to strike a deal. He'd buy it in exchange for a hug, during which he whispered in my ear how bright I was. His hands, unblemished, clasped too tightly and lingered on what hips I had, still four feet tall.

I had no compelling argument for this fox, whose red fur thins at his temples. Why expend the energy explaining yourself to someone who is always right?

I walked him to the door quietly, watching as he draped the scarf over his shoulders. Why wear it if not to bring you warmth?

When we stepped onto the porch and were out of the party's sight, he wrapped me in a tight hug. I did not cry. Nor did I as he walked away. He did not look back.

Eventually, I did show my mother the scar on my hand. She cried and insisted, if she had known, she'd have repaired the rotting fence ages ago. We don't live in that house anymore, but the fence still stands. On quiet days, I drive past it to see if the peas still grow. The fox is never there. Sometimes, during conversations which have little to do with that old life of ours, my mother will suddenly announce, "Isn't it good that he stopped coming around? We never had to tell him to, he just did. On his own volition." I don't know if it's good. I don't know if I'll ever stop driving past the old house to see if he changed his mind.

When this fox, the one who put on wire-rimmed sunglasses as he walked down the sidewalk, faded into the horizon, I turned on my heel and entered the party once more. I did not talk to anyone on my way to the wooden table in the back. I did not look at them. I served myself a plate and walked right back out the door. I sat on the brick stoop with my legs uncrossed, quite unladylike. As I adjusted myself to get comfortable, my stockings caught on the uneven caulking. I did not fawn over the rip, I tucked into my meal. I picked the cranberries and walnuts out of the salad first and placed each leaf into my mouth gingerly with my thumb and forefinger. I spooned the stew over the rice and, when it was done, sopped up the boozy, fatty liquid with a chunk of bread. I ate my slice of pie with a great towering dollop of whipped cream.

It was a start.

Tits
Dalanie Beach

I am twelve years old, turning to one side before the mirror in my mom's bathroom, running a hand down my body, from sternum to stomach: willing it all *flat*.

I am fourteen years old, running across the front lawn toward my grandmother's car to shout something at her before she pulls out of the driveway. As I trot back up to the house, my mom narrows her eyes at my bouncing chest, scrutinizing the little teepees my nipples now form under my shirt. She scoffs, "You're too old to run around without a bra."

I am fifteen years old, flipping with a cautious sort of interest through a magazine article targeted at teenage girls, titled "Make Peace with Your Boobs!" and trying, like the good little Catholic girl I've been raised to be, to swallow down my disgust long enough to think such a thing is possible.

I am eighteen years old, dressed in the see-through, uniform shirt of my high school, resting my head on my desk, when a tall boy I barely know well enough to dislike snickers, "I like your pink zebra-stripe bra."

I am twenty-three years old, lying on my partner's bed, trying to understand the feeling the poster of a shirtless K-Pop idol is stirring awake inside me. It's an achy, burning feeling. Not desire. Not attraction. More like… envy. I want that scrawny boy's chest. Or more accurately, I want the freedom, the relief, the *rightness* that a chest like that could afford me.

I am twenty-four years old, standing before the mirror in the first apartment I share with my partner. Beige-colored tape holds my chest down, compressing it into something almost affirming, almost me. It's shocking how much of a difference the tape makes. The person in the mirror is so tantalizingly close to how I feel inside. Half-relieved, with hot tears gathering, I turn to the side. A cold gut-punch of dysphoria. Tape and binders can only do so much to hide my useless mammary tissue, which cannot be removed safely without surgery, and the brutal reminder of this fact sends me over the edge. I turn on the bathroom fan and sob.

I am twenty-five years old, listening to the words my mother allegedly said after I had confessed to her that I wanted to pursue top-surgery (chest masculinization surgery) as a permanent solution to my dysphoria. "How dare she [my mother does not respect my pronouns] want this surgery when there are women with breast cancer who don't have a choice?"

This response, transphobic in the worst way, also follows a cruel, nonsensical line of logic that my partner later pointed out: "You might as well say, 'How dare your mom have five kids when there are people in the world who can't have children? How dare your mom live in a house when there are homeless people in the world? How dare your mom eat food when there are people starving?'"

I have craved the relief of a flat chest since before I could articulate it, before I knew the difference between sex and gender, before I understood what trans meant, before I had thought deeply enough about my own subscription to gender roles to challenge their gross inaccuracies and injustices.

It will be a painful and invasive surgery, with a lengthy recovery time, and I would not be pursuing it if I didn't want it with all I am.

I think about it every day. I cannot dress, shower, undress, pass a mirror, or move in a way that sets them in motion without wanting it: to be, for the rest of my life, without tits.

Favorite Flower
Nanami Fetter

The very first thing I noticed about the past, was that there were fewer buildings. That, and the fact that the world felt cooler. The summer, less hot. Other than that, it was the same. To me, seemingly, not much had changed in terms of the way people acted or had always been.

Whoever decided that only white flowers were appropriate for a service didn't consider the fact that the person dying may have had a favorite flower, and would've liked to be buried in those instead. But at her funeral, my mother was covered in many white chrysanthemums. When her favorites were actually marigolds.

"Inori," my grandmother called.

I stood at the entrance of the funeral hall, shuffling off my sneakers. Instead of a black dress, I had worn my bright yellow one that my mother had made me the year before. The sleeves were slightly too tight, but I didn't care. It was the first time I was wearing it.

I sat down at the very front of the aisle, right in front of her casket. The Buddhist monks glanced over at me slightly, but didn't say a word. My other family members were silent. Then, gently, I felt my grandfather's hand on my shoulder.

"Don't worry," he said quietly. "This will all be over soon."

Perhaps he was talking about the actual funeral itself. But to me it sounded like he was talking about something else.

I nodded. Then sat perfectly still as the monks sent my mother's spirit off towards the afterlife.

—

Standing in front of our family grave always made me nervous. I was worried that my relatives would be able to hear my thoughts, or that they were always looking at me in disapproval.

"Say hello," my mother would always say when we would visit. But I always found it strange to talk to a tombstone, whether it contained my ancestor's ashes or not. Still, after my mother died, I didn't feel nervous in front of their graves anymore.

Washing the grave was always my favorite part. I could do it in silence and not have to worry about what I was going to say or pray about. But it was then that I found my surroundings begin to change. Or perhaps, it was me who had changed, not the world.

Pouring the water down over the headstone, suddenly the sun began to shine on my back. I turned around and found that the old tree in the corner of the graveyard was gone. Only a dirty spot remained where it had been, even though moments ago, there had been shade. At first, I thought it was just an illusion.

Was the tree never there? But then why? I stood there for a moment staring at the spot the old tree used to stand, and then wondered if I had just imagined it.

Perhaps in my grief, I was forgetting things, I thought. It wouldn't be so unusual to me.

And so in my daze, I began to walk around the graveyard, heading toward the exit after giving the ancestor's gravestone a good scrub. And lighting some incense. I skipped the prayer with just the clapping of my hands. I didn't have anything to say.

Next, it was the cars. The cars were all different shapes and colors. Simply put, they were vintage. It was audibly noticeable, and yet I convinced myself it was normal. Maybe there had just happened to be older cars on the road that day. All the while, I thought this to myself, and then pulled out my phone.

It was annoying that I couldn't use it. Just for a little bit. I always figured I was pretty addicted to my phone, but I got used to it after a while. The only thing was that it made me more aware of my surroundings, and I hated that.

Like how suddenly, the sounds of almost everything made my head turn and made me want to observe it. Like the sound of electricity buzzing through telephone poles, birds in the distance, or the sound of me swallowing my own spit repeatedly. I was looking for a vending machine or a convenience store to buy some bottled water.

I walked like this for hours, and yet there was no sign of any store. Just miles and miles of neighborhood.

—

My father's hair was frizzy and dyed. Seemingly sun bleached. I found him at his parent's house, or rather, down by the beach with a surfboard. It took a while for him to notice me, as he kept going back to the waves and then back again. It seemed like hours before I could actually get to talk to him, and even longer for him to understand why I was there.

"So, what's the future look like?"

"Bleak. And scary."

"Ah, well, I suppose that's obvious."

I looked over at him and then back down at the sand. We were sitting on some driftwood that was scratching at my legs, and not comfortable at all. I would've preferred we had stood, but my father had sat down and I had followed suit, not wanting him to go anywhere.

"It's true. It looks like the end is closer than you might think."

"Wait, really?"

He looked over at me, and then took a deep breath in.

"Seriously?"

I nodded.

"That is pretty grim. I didn't think you were so pessimistic."

I smiled, knowing he was just entertaining me. He didn't really believe that I was from the future. I had nothing to prove who I really was.

"And the future is hotter," I said.

"Why's that?"

"The world is getting hotter from fossil fuel emissions. It all gets trapped in the atmosphere I think, which makes the earth hotter."

"Hmm…"

"It's science."

"I'm a humanities sort of guy."

"So am I."

"So it's way past us, huh?"

"Yup."

"Even if I try to understand it, I just don't," I said.

"But you can accept it, right?" he said. "You don't have to understand to be able to accept something the way it is."

"I can't do it…"

My throat dried up. I felt thirsty all over again. Reaching over to my side, I took a sip from my water bottle.

"I get it," my father said. "I can't accept anything either. I want to take everything that's in my hands and crush it. Tightly, so that it doesn't escape sometimes."

That makes you a bad person, I wanted to say, but didn't have the courage to. I was always afraid of making other people angry at me. And I didn't really believe it. Despite everything, I didn't think I was a better person than my father.

My father then took out a cigarette and began to smoke it.

"I didn't know you smoked," I accidentally said out loud.

"You don't know me," my father said, laughing.

"That's true," I said, leaning back.

The smoke felt ticklish in my lungs, making me cough.

—

Usually, I never fought with my mother. I had always felt that I was a pretty obedient child who wasn't too much trouble to raise. And yet sometimes, there were moments when I wanted to lash out at her, and so I did.

I don't remember exactly what it was that I said, which was unusual for me. I usually always remembered words, whether it was others or my own. Rather than their actions, or the feelings that I was feeling, or the feelings of others. My memory failed me in all those ways.

The only thing I remembered was the shape and color of my words, and the general feeling of what I was trying to say. Essentially, I was yelling at her that everything was all her fault, and that she was supposed to understand me better. I ended up yelling at her for forty minutes straight, all the while she stared at me in silence. My throat was an awful wreck afterwards, but I did feel a whole lot better in my chest. I was finally able to get all the words out, and I was elated. The only thing I feared was retaliation.

Three days later, I went up to her and hugged my mother tightly. I didn't know how to apologize. I had never been taught how to, and I didn't want to learn anytime soon.

"Where did you go?" my mother asked me, hugging me back.

I didn't answer. Just kept clinging to her.

—

The sounds of frogs at night sting me. Sometimes the smell of rain and plants moves me when I recognize it. When it's something I remember smelling before, I'm quickly moved to tears. It'll feel like a long time since I've experienced anything.

I want to enjoy my life too, you know? I want to not be afraid and laugh. But somewhere along the way, I became unable to even do that. I think I chose to be unhappy because it made the most sense. It hurt me a lot less to do that than to be genuine. No matter what, I can't properly face people. Especially myself.

Sometimes I can smell the exact smell that's causing me to remember, and then I try to soak it in. I stand very still and wait for it to leave me, not the other way around. And every time, I'm afraid that it's never going to come back. My mother had a smell like that.

But if I hold her clothes tightly, I'll burst into tears. Which is why I had to give them a good wash beforehand. The day she died, I realized I would have to forget all about her.

Every action I've taken since then has been in order to accomplish that.

It's become my main goal.

—

I found my mother at her university's campus by asking

around for her. It took a little while to find the building she was teaching in, but there she was. Her hair that was usually tied up in my memories was down and messy. I walked up to her and pretended to look for the bathroom.

"All the way over there," she said, pointing her finger and closing one eye. She stretched her words out as she spoke and pointed for a long time. I looked in the direction of her finger and then finally gave up and thanked her. It wasn't like I had expected her to know me, but the thought of having to explain my arrival made me tired just thinking about it.

If I called your name now, there's no way you'd recognize it, right? I thought. Either way, I guessed it didn't matter. I wouldn't be calling her name anytime soon. In real life, or my dreams. I was so sure of it.

"You're very pretty," she said the next time we met.

I must've blushed or looked embarrassed, because she then smiled as though she knew what was going on.

"Are you dating someone?"

"Not at all."

"Are you married?"

"I don't ever want to get married."

"You never know," my mother said.

"You never know," I said. "About anything."

"I've got a boyfriend now," my mother said. "And he's the one."

I sucked in hot air through my teeth. Even though I knew it was a stupid conversation, I had to change the subject somehow.

"I wanted to tell you something actually," I said. "Can you take this to heart?"

My mother leaned forward to listen, just like she always did in the future.

"You can't get married to him," I told her. "You can't have children. You can't have a daughter, and then get killed by your husband. Your daughter would want you to be happy, and not regret things. She wouldn't want to exist in a world where you weren't happy. There wouldn't be any point."

My mother looked at me for a moment, frowning. Then shook her head.

"You have a weird way of worrying about someone," she said. "I can grasp my own happiness, you know? It's in my own hands, not my daughter's, or anyone else's. That doesn't make any sense anyhow. No one knows what's going to happen a minute from now, or way far out into the future. That's not something anyone can control."

I felt hopelessness in my chest when she said that. Then wiped the sweat from my forehead. My mother took out a pale yellow handkerchief and then handed it to me.

"It's hot this year, isn't it?" my mother said, smiling again. She seemed to have forgotten entirely about our conversation. "It'd be nice to go to the beach in weather like this, wouldn't it?"

I couldn't answer her. At that point, my heart had completely shriveled up and dried out.

after another's arm
Lorelei Bacht

after alive, after another's arm, a turn-
around – but not as beautiful.

a bell begins to blink our bodies into view,
come blue curtains of dawn.

after capable of action comes desire
now diminished, fraction   of a familiar

glow, holding. if an impulse, the nature of
this beast: *is it   or isn't it?*

tree branch once liveable, now made
matches.   might we more of morning?

i name myself, and the naming nervous.
   the checklist reads: *none. or nothing.*

if only the right ring, if only shapes stopped
   still. if only the bird kept its tongue –

a tenderness? a *we,*   a *what,*   a *whatever.*

did we dream the wind's delicate

weavework in the frangipani? afterwards:
i will walk the world.   not yours.   but mine.

a recipe for disaster
Lorelei Bacht

a daffodil,
but make it white
and paint its heart
apricot red.

tell it: *you are*
nothing. now go
tell the others
the same.

spread it:
black marmalade,
sugar burnt at
the bottom of the pan.

what says
you were right
better than
i am the same?

and so, i grow
a white collar,

a frill of grandiosity
to mask

the mess of burnt
apricot jam
you made and called
whatever the nametag

on my yellow coat said.

the house we will not build
Lorelei Bacht

all anchors abandoned. between asked
    and answered: a bridge,   broken.

calling for clouds, i trip on ceramic –
its discolored, sharp archaeology

spells *difficult*, spells *deficit*, evens out
every fall: what does, doesn't.   each

tree abandoned to its failing figs, its cut
fingers. no hand to hold the hole now

   bright. beneath the leaf a little loss
lingers, meaning more mouth, but

miserable, and managing nothing.
it occupies the past, the pearls once piled,

now poured without purpose. i'd rather
reach reason. revoke the rib of its season.

   something else requires to stand

and sail through this wildness, outgrown:

all i want from life is a while that works.

Weather Vane
Cassady O'Reilly-Hahn

on the roof, a rooster shreds
wind like a grind rail
at the skate park. Bad bitch.
He ollies east-west until

all that wind blows out from under him
and I realize I have been staring
too long at the neighbor's house
for someone out walking their dog

in the rain. I am a lightning rod
for gossip, the blade of light
at a coffee table of darkness.
I don't need Mrs. Wallace to drop her curtain

and pick up the chunk of landline
she keeps on the side table, smile, and
whip back around, even if the rooster
is rocking a sick double 900.

My Short Life as a White Trash Debutante

Mary Elise Myers

The year I moved to San Francisco from Boston, I wanted to disappear–fly into the ethereal–which was funny because this city is called "the Land of the Living." There is not one graveyard in its foggy jurisdiction. If you wanted or needed to die—you could take the BART to Marin County or Oakland or get reincarnated as a moth when visiting UC Berkeley with the help of the Student Unions' Transcendental Meditation Club.

    I was accepted into the San Francisco State's Master of Arts program. And although I devoured books, I hated literature class. Although I loved writing stories about angry violent feminist who were incarcerated for burning lingerie stores, I despised analyzing the Shakespearean Prologues and Thomas Hardy's novel *Far from the Maddening Crowd* which my New England College forced me to dissect two times for two different courses because it was good for me. I passed with Cs.

    So, San Francisco State allowed me into graduate writing program on one condition: I needed higher Literature grades and therefore more undergraduate credits including the dreadful *Moby Dick*. Thank God, in the Castro section of town, *Moby Dick* was also a bar where I could drink myself to death.

I lived in the Mission. I shared an unheated loft with four other people and managed to financially survive as a coffee attendant at the FBI building downtown across from the IRS office. Every morning at five-thirty, I walked through a metal detector and entered a tiny room without windows. There was only one counter and an espresso machine and bags of coffee stored on the unwashed floor. Our goal was to caffeinate government workers to incur adequate mental function.

The only break from Melville and the torturous essays on Ahab's megalomania as well as the timely chore of satisfying tax men and women with tubs of unrestricted caffeine was as a volunteer at a women's experimental theater on Valencia Street. At this venue, I ripped tickets and showed people to their seats as women in tattoos and piercings sang the blues or belly danced for the evening's performance. I often dreamed of jumping on stage and wondered what it would be like to be the second coming of Patty Smith—singing about a broken heart in a man's world.

But despite my classes, work and daily walks through Golden Gate Park, I was lonely. The university had 40,000 strangers, my roommates worked full-time and the women at the theater were cliquish, preferring female trapeze artists to plain Bostonian me.

So, after buying a tempeh salad at the Natural Foods Store, I approached a large community board hoping to find a friend or at least divergence from syllabi, because, I believed, these cork bulletin boards contained magical powers–a portal to a better place in life which held postings for roommates, maids, drum circles, Heavy Metal knitting for singles, organic childcare, improvisation groups with an emphasis on Kabuki theater and organ donations.

Finally, underneath layers and layers of black and white posters, ads, tags and listings there was a band flier photocopied haphazardly–spotted with lint hairs caught under the fierce light of a Xerox machine.

> **Back-up Singer Wanted:** Are you naturally social, chatty and like to dance? Do you sing in the shower or at least at your cousin's bar mitzvah after having one too many drinks? Do you like to listen to the Ramones, Blondie, New York Dolls and the Sex Pistols? Are you sick of the system? Call Gigi Goat if you wanna be sedated and sing in the legendary Punk Rock band The White Trash Debutantes.

I answered yes to ad's questionnaire except for the bar mitzvah one since most of my Jewish friends growing up were atheists. I wasn't sure what type of horrible system Gigi Goat was referring to but if thrashing involved fighting for women's equality or at least allowing professors to assign books by women (fuck whales) then I was ready to jump on stage and rant about sexist iambic pentameter. Maybe I'd write a song about my love for Amy Tan or Toni Morrison. "We need to get Toni in the Literary Canon! Up Yours!" Then I imagined slam dancing in-between choruses and dreamed of changing the conscious minds of the literary world one thrown beer can at a time.

When I finally called Mrs. or Ms. Goat, I was pleasantly surprised by her enthusiasm since there were people, I had imagined, more qualified in the entertainment industry than me. Admittedly, I was never in an actual musical group. I was, however, in a high school jazz band where I played the theme from the TV show "Dynasty" on my clarinet.

"All I need to know is if you like Punk?" Gigi breathed deeply into the phone. "You know your Punk?"

"Do I know my Punk? I listened to The Clash when I was seven!" I proudly declared. "My favorite movie is Decline of Western Civilization! My country is Black Flag! I went to a Bikini Kill concert and jumped in a mosh pit and got punched in the face."

Cosmic Studios' practice space was on Folsom Street across from the health food store—a ten-minute walk from my loft. I was glad to escape the severe warmth of my colossal room, which was half the size of a basketball court. One would think huge urban spaces would be desirable as most apartments in the area were immeasurably tiny but due to lack of insulation and weak protection from the penetrating California sun, my bedroom was truly inhabitable. I was basically residing in a shelled-out warehouse that was once a sex club from the 70s.

As I entered Cosmic's lobby, I found myself encased in zigzagged pinewood paneling (ceiling to walls) reminiscent of past basement installations where I played canasta with my best friend as a child. The dirt brown rug was stained and unwelcoming prompting my own doubtful-uncertain feelings towards Gigi Goat or, for that matter, The White Trash Debutantes. I pondered on the term "white trash"—an offensive name for poor Caucasians. I could reassure myself that the band's name was tongue-in-cheek and still the label was unsettling which, unfortunately, made it more tempting for me to explore this title—to embrace its viciousness and to become its caricature—to show how simplistic and asinine it was thereby proving a Punk Rock point.

Finally, a woman in a lavender leotard pushed through the glass doors that eventually lead into the studio practice space. She wore black leather motorcycle boots and fishnet stockings. An opaque white scarf was tied around her neck. A ruby tiara held up her dark brown Nancy Sinatra hair—lacquered and intimidatingly voluminous.

"I would be careful if I were you," she barked as she pulled out a little mirror and applied cherry red lipstick to her dry lips. "That couch has lice."

In the studio room, the soundproof walls were covered in soft gray foamy material like the mattress my grandmother slept on to relieve her sciatica. There was a skinny man with short blonde hair on drums; the guitar player's long black hair fell to the floor as he held his blue Fender–up against a sequenced red jumpsuit. Gigi said his name was Larry and he was "fucking amazing." There wasn't a bass player. The last one quit due to artistic differences.

"He felt uncomfortable calling the Queen of England a fascist? Apparently, he's from Dorset," explained the drummer.

"You'll love the girls," Gigi smiled.

When the girls did arrive, they pushed through the door with two bottles of tequila over their heads. One wore a tight black dress and carried a toy pistol on a holster around her waist. The other girl was a redhead and lengthy–a model from an L.L. Bean catalog that unknowingly wandered into a Social Distortion concert. She introduced herself as Cindy the flight attendant. That was her real job. Cindy was engaged to a millionaire who lived in North Beach, and I would be replacing her as a backup singer since she wouldn't return after her elaborate wedding on Catalina Island. The other one just drank from her bottle wiping her face with the back of her hand. She said her name was Kat and that she could kick really high.

"It's just a bunch of BULL SHIT!" she shouted as I shook her hand during introductions.

The first song the band practiced was "Little Eddie"—an ode to a man who could deliver in bed despite being a short-statured person. I soon learned that I had to become comfortable with expressing aspects of the male anatomy in all its incarnations such as chanting out phallic phrases over brutal guitar distortion and snare rolls. Ultimately, *love a man for his penis size*, should be as easy to scream on stage as *Somewhere Over the Rainbow*. But somehow it was not.

Gigi sang lead, of course. Her "singing" bridged genres or at least time and space. It was a cross between unrhymed rap and a disgruntled passenger on a plane complaining about inadequate legroom. It worked in *the I don't care what you think, it's all a government conspiracy* sort of way. Fortunately, the band had *Larry the fucking amazing guitar player* whose trills drowned out Gigi's vocal imperfections or at least the loud squawks from the leggy Cindy and Kat.

The next number they practiced was "Susan Lucci." Ms. Lucci's inability to win an Emmy in the Daytime Television Category was an abomination to Ms. Goat. Gigi proudly wrote the lyrics and the 3 chords (G, E and D).

"And people said we weren't political." Gigi smiled then lit a cigarette, which she referred to as her *herbal tea cleanse.*

During the short intermission, I approached Gigi (who was now spraying her hair with a large can of what looked like bug repellent) and mentioned how the band might pay tribute to other strong American women.

"I mean, Susan Lucci's great but ... what about ... Emma Goldman ... Harriet Tubman ... Sojourner Truth ... Gertrude Stein."

"What record labels are they on?" Gigi inhaled.

Before I went home, Cindy pulled me over to the Marshall Stacks.

"Listen. You aren't glamorous—not like me and Kat," she said, looking over to where her singing partner had passed out in the corner, "but you are all right. Gigi thinks everyone needs to dress provocatively even at a funeral–especially at a funeral. I mean, she wears leotards. Okay boas. But that's it. Even in the rain season and trust me it gets cold in San Fran during the California monsoons. She always wants to look like an outrageous kitten and she needs to realize that not everyone is sexy. But you can sing and I wish that would be enough. But you're in…just wear something slutty to the next band practice. Okay."

"Okay." I owned mostly overalls. "I'll try."

*

Life went on as usual, which dampened my excitement as an honoree member of The White Trash Debutant. Gigi held practice every Monday and Thursday for the past month but I still woke up at five in the morning and took the BART to the FBI building to serve overpriced coffee. I still volunteered on Friday nights to rip tickets on Valencia Street for the new show "the Last Feminists on Earth"—a juggling extravaganza. I still attended my American Literature class. We were now on Hawthorne. It was odd how I had moved to the west coast expecting to read something transformative by the Beat Writers or by Maxine Hong Kingston. And yet, here I was decoding the significance of New England clam chowder and Witch Burning. Either way, I had a routine to my life.

And finally, my first night of a gig came. I headed to the club and went over my chants: *Penis, Lucci, USA, Superstar, Fucked Up Car,* and *She's the Boss.* I didn't really know how to dance so instead I planned on doing a series of elaborate jumping jacks on stage. I was ready. And real. I was sick of the fake. As a Literature student I pretended to care about poetic Puritans gathering acorns in the forest. As a coffee attendant I pretended to care about my tired customers "half cafs" or "slim lattes." As a woman's improvisational theatre volunteer, I pretended the performers had talent. Yet, at *The Bottom of the Hill Bar and Grille*, I would be myself—pure Punk Rock. Raging originality. That's what I thought. That's what I believed.

When I arrived at the club, Gigi was already at the bar doing tequila shots and sucking on limes. She shook her shellacked dark brown hair. A delicate golden tiara was bobby pinned into her head. She called me over enthusiastically with one loud, "Biiiiiittttchhh!"

By her side was a plastic Safeway shopping bag, which struck me as odd since she seemed more of a leopard print suitcase type. She pulled out a light blue bejeweled tutu. Anna Pavlova would be proud.

"Go put this on in the bathroom and don't fuck it up. I got this at Ed Asner's yard sale. Vintage shit." She knocked back another drink. "Oh, did I tell you. You get paid for shows. Sometimes in beers and sometimes in cash but tonight you're gonna see some green, honey."

I forgot to bring pantyhose or fishnets stocking but luckily I shaved myself down to the clitoris—in case my legs would be examined under floodlights or a surgeon's table. As I walked out of the bathroom stall with my tutu on, which fit remarkably well, there was Gigi smoking a cigarette partaking in her *tea cleanse* next to the garbage can.

"Where's your fucking make-up?" she asked and blew smoke in my face—then pushed me against the sink with her chest. A switch. No more affectionate *biiiiitch*.

Just down to business ramming me against pink ceramic.

"I don't own any make-up." I swallowed (a shameful confession for a stage performer). "I didn't think I needed any. Patti Smith doesn't wear any."

"Patti Smith. You think you've got HER cheekbones. This is 'Debutant' territory. We are provocateurs. Burlesque throwbacks filled with temptation and lust." She turned towards her plastic bag and finally pulled out: pancake make-up, red lipstick, frosted pink eye shadow, eyeliner and blue mascara. "Emergency Stash." She rubbed foundation all over my face. I was her Pygmalion. "Guys need to dream about having sex with you."

"What if I don't like guys?" I challenged. "Or maybe I like both?"

"Then whoever ya like, moron. There might be a biker chic waiting for you or Harry S. Truman but no one will be there if you look like a piano teacher from the St. Angus of Rome parish."

Up on the stage, Kat was practicing her kicks. She wore a see-through mesh top, which revealed two tassels covering each nipple. She lifted her long fishnet clad leg and then, from under her loose hamstring, pulled the gun's trigger. A small red flag popped out. "Bang!"

The crowd was thin. But according to Gigi, it was a Tuesday and not everyone partied every day of the week like she did.

"Let's be thankful we could even play in a legendary club. This is an honor." Ginger jumped on stage and grabbed the mike. "We still don't have a bass player."

The crowd sighed in sympathy. A man raised his

hand and said he could play but Ginger told him he needed to audition first because what did it think the band was a fucking local church choir.

When I got on stage, the spotlight burned the top of my head. I looked like an eleven-year-old in the tutu. I felt like an eleven-year-old in a tutu. The make-up irritated my skin. A man in a cowboy hat and yellow t-shirt studied me—his estranged wife from Reno now found in a Punk club.

Joe the drummer took his place behind his set. Larry, the guitarist, lifted his instrument from the stand and held his guitar up high on his chest. He had on black lingerie–his flat chest slightly exposed above the lace. After Joe counted to five the band started the song, "Susan Lucci." Gigi belted out the sorrowful story as I tried chanting into the microphone. But something overcame me. Intense humiliation–a propped up corpse whose one talent was staring at a bowl of peanuts that rested on the bar.

When "Susan Lucci" was finished, Gigi marched my way clicking her heels against hard wood.

"You need to dance, girly." She pushed two fingers into my side then snapped the back of my bra with her sharp claws. "Move your fucking ass. And try to sing a little."

"Listen to your momma." The man in the cowboy hat advised—a self-appointed family counselor with a bottle of gin.

But, when Larry began the next number on a low chord, I couldn't budge. I only mumbled silence. A standing coma.

Ms. Goat called for a quick intermission. She dragged me to the pink tiled bathroom to have a little conference. Kat looked at me as if witnessing her own death.

"Sit down on the toilet." Gigi demanded. "Let's talk, butterfly. Listen. I want you to really shake it up out there because if you don't … I am gonna kick your ass and I am twice as big as you and I am not afraid of jail." Gigi pointed her nails into my glittered abdomen.

She left me alone hyperventilating by an empty toilet roll. All I wanted was to embrace myself as a piece of ironical trash. I bought the body revealing clothing that Cindy the flight attendant suggested. I acquired the miniskirts and half shirts and the platform shoes with money that should have gone to rent. I wore these outfits all the time, now. Could I be a woman who used sexiness as a statement of her own liberation? But in my heart, I dreamed of my desk where I analyzed Phillis Wheatley poems, or curled up with a book about Marie Curie, or walked the Mission as the moon drifted up into the night sky—a dear, wild daughter of the wolves.

So, lacking any type of medical insurance, I went back on the stage, and performed my fifty jumpy jacks and leaped in the air to chants of penis. I gave the cowboy a show he wouldn't forget. He threw his hat in the air as Kat shot her toy gun under her strong leg. "Boom!" Someone in the back of room shouted "Smurf girl" and "Muppet girl." I wasn't real. This wasn't real. The drummer broke his sticks and the guitar player stripped down to his shorts—casually throwing his black nightie into the small crowd. And Gigi rolled around on the stage until her crown became lopsided. Her boa wound up so tightly around her neck that she began an uncontrollable coughing fit. It just added to the madness that entertained the braindead fans that came for the show. Part of me hoped she choked to death in her leotard.

As I gathered my things to leave (still in the Ed Asner yard sale's vintage tutu) a smiling Gigi approached me.

"I wasn't gonna really kick your ass, you know. It was a joke. Take your money," she insisted. I held out my hand and, in my palm, Gigi Goat placed an old damp five-dollar bill, ripped then scotched taped through President Abraham Lincoln's depressed expression.

"You earned it," she gleamed then lit a cigarette making circles around her Nancy Sinatra hair. "Every penny of it!"

At two in the morning, cars honked at me as I headed home. A blue convertible slowed down. The driver, a man with long dark hair, asked me if I needed a ride. It was the guitarist, now in his silk lingerie. He tossed his cigarette onto the tar. I got in. We sped up the hill on a treeless road. When I stepped out of his car, I watched him fly into darkness as I moved along the sidewalk heading to my loft, still in vintage tutu. In the neon shadows, when I lifted my arms towards the stars, it appeared as if I had grown wings. The pavement lit brightly under my combat boots. And then there was that astonishing whiteness of the moon—a whale laughing and singing, dancing and dreaming above me—swimming in the blackness of a vast ocean of California sky.

Lindy Bird Fly
Melissa Rotert

Lindy dreamed of birds and balloons, clouds and Cessnas, anything that could take her away from the ground and into the sky. What can one expect from a child named after an aviation great? But it wasn't her namesake that drew her inexorably towards flight. For that, she owed her father. Walter "Wingless" Marshall flew helicopters for the Navy long before Lindy landed in his life. Two years before her birth, Walter was permanently grounded and honorably discharged following a crash that left him half a leg down.

He came home to his young wife and put his time in the skies behind him. Walter didn't want to talk about it with anyone. That was, until his little Lindy Bird was born. He shared with her the secrets of his life on high: daring missions of rescue, storms that froze his rotor blades, and tales of camaraderie in his squadron. Lindy would perch on her father's good knee and listen for hours, never seeing him smile so brightly as he did in those stolen moments. It was only natural that she would spend her days, head in the clouds, searching for her father's joy.

Seven-year-old Lindy had finally plucked up the courage to climb out of the attic window and onto the highest branch of the mighty oak that shaded her front yard. All summer she'd cycled through plan after meticulous flight plan for a way to safely land at the bottom and share her adventure in the skies with Walter. Lindy was certain her father would beam so full of pride that he'd forget to stop smiling. She'd cut flimsy cardboard wings and tied balloons around her waist, but nothing seemed flightworthy. Having run out of ideas, Lindy snuck into the attic with a flashlight after supper. It was her father's poker night and her mother was covering a night shift at the diner. Little Lindy Bird was certain that if she could just find her father's old military memorabilia—the one thing she was forbidden from touching in the dusty crawl space—then she would discover the secret to a successful flight.

Lindy found the worn leather-skinned trunk that held Walter's treasures and set to searching through the contents, respectfully displacing those that would not aid her mission. Under a pile of documents and love letters from her mother, her fingers thrilled at the crinkle of paper packaging. Carefully lifting it from the base of the large trunk, Lindy wondered why this bundle alone had been so tenderly packed away. She'd discovered medals in small cases and her father's old dress uniform tossed haphazardly into storage. Even the tiny set of wings she so admired in the photos of Walter that hung on her grandmother's rose-papered walls was loose within the box. Whatever her father hid within the delicate brown paper and thin cord of twine must mean something special to him.

Every time Lindy moved the package she feared the boisterous crackle of starched paper would call attention to her invasion of Walter's past. But with each pause, her betrayal went undiscovered. Delicately, Lindy Bird pulled the knot from the twine and parted the paper folds to reveal a wooden box. She gulped at the fortitude necessary to go one step more for an answer, feeling in her bones that the secret to flying lay within. Lifting the lid, Lindy frowned at the crumpled mass of nylon that revealed itself in the silvery light. It wasn't until she unfurled the lightweight fabric that she realized what she held. The object in her hands was both a parachute and the answer to her problem.

Impatient to try, Lindy used the twine to tie the parachute around her thin torso. If either parent discovered her disloyalty to her father, breaking his one rule, she would never be allowed to return to the attic. Her flight test became an emergency operation. The very idea of it tingled with electricity up her small spine. It took some doing to pry open the paint-sealed dormer frame, but eventually her window for takeoff was clear.

Stepping out carefully onto the heavy wooden branch, Lindy had not anticipated the wind. Nor had she expected her father's head to crest above the narrow stairway that led to the attic. No small feat for a one-legged man.

"Lindy!" Walter called in panicked desperation as the chute began to billow in the evening breeze, rippling with desire to take off. Her grinning face turned in delight to see the sheer terror on her father's face. There was no smile of pride as she expected. Only helplessness and fear. "Lindy!" he shouted again, as she lifted off the branch in a harsh jolt backwards into the dimming blue sky.

Lindy didn't know the importance of the parachute. She couldn't have guessed why her father had put so much care into preserving such a strange relic of his military days. Little Lindy Bird didn't know that when Walter "Wingless" Marshall was shot from the sky, the nylon sail had saved his life. Walter didn't know if it might save hers too.

Encoded
Lucian McDowell

CDG – JFK – PIT | 1988

In my memory I open the front door and there you stand in the December night, smiling in your white button-down shirt and Burberry blazer. But that can't be right. I must have come to pick you up at the airport myself, then brought you home, giddy during introductions, my father, bluff and hearty, squashing your hand. How peculiar things must have seemed to you, the Parisian writer, that to me were as familiar as my hand. The dark hills. The sleeping town. The big red brick house. The friendly panting yellow dog. Because we were not married, you were given my childhood bedroom, with its light blue carpet and flowered wallpaper. I slept down the hall in my brother's old room. Pan Am 103 had exploded over Lockerbie the day before. It felt like a very close call. It made your arrival sweeter.

CDG – JFK – MSY | 1989

You were doing research on jazz for an article for a glossy French magazine. I was that grinning goggled dog in the sidecar, happily along for the ride. The trip was paid for by the magazine. It felt delicious, like we were getting away with something. This was the second stop in a five-city, ten-day tour. At the airport Hilton we stayed in the room while you read and wrote. We ordered mozzarella sticks and hamburgers and wore bathrobes thick as mink coats. We had no money, only your expense account, but we felt like rock stars. Eventually we took a cab into the French Quarter so you could interview an aged drummer at the Café Napoléon with its pocked plaster, sultry air, Caribbean-style decrepitude. Afterward, we happened into a restaurant crammed with lively people at long tables. According to their red T-shirts, they were celebrating Chester Zardis's 90th birthday. We didn't know Chester Zardis, but we bought a T-shirt and wedged ourselves among them and ate gumbo while a local jazz band played. Back at the hotel, someone had left chocolates on the pillows and a small folded sign that said *Rêve bien.*

ORD – MCI | 1989

In the desk drawer of the room, a postcard showed the motel in 1969, an ugly ochre-colored column planted in a parking lot. Twenty years later, it was unchanged. I ordered a cheese omelet. When it arrived on a tray placed outside our door, I lifted the round plastic lid and found an eggy half-moon sweating under a lurid triangle of Velveeta. But hey, it was room service. I sat on the edge of the bed and ate it while you made notes for the day. Later we somehow made our way into the right city. Wandering up and down 18th and Vine, I conjured the ghosts of the famous tap-dancing brothers. I could see them rising in unison, their bodies tilted, clicking their heels in a perfect O before their legs sprang out straight again, like a pair of wishbones, could see them run up the muralled walls and do backflips, the broken glass crunching when they landed. We had dinner in a steak house. We were Lewis and Clark. With you I was discovering America.

JFK – RKV + CDG – RKV | 1986

This was before me, during the death throes of your life with B, who by then had spent much of the royalties from your bestseller on shoes. During your blistering arguments, she would threaten to defenestrate herself. After you told me this I was often visited by the image of her silhouette in a tall window frame, a lifesize X. In my mind I heard the shrill, empty threat: *Je vais sauter!* During this time that was before me, you were still in New York but she had gone back to Paris. To renegotiate your relationship, she demanded a summit here, like Reagan and Gorbachev's a few months before. New York, Paris … I see your two planes landing, like arms crossing, on the moonscape runways. At least you got a pair of locally made sweaters out of it, though I never could bring myself to wear one. B was so present in our early days, calling in the night from across the Atlantic, a plaintive voice creeping along undersea cables and into your ear. One day a big box arrived in the mail. She had sent you a grease-coated toaster oven full of rubber bands. I pretended

B didn't bother me, but her existence ate me alive. When you went to work I would take her old student ID card out of your drawer and make myself look at this face that had mattered to you before mine.

CDG – IAD | 1989

I don't remember why we landed here, since our wedding was a four-hour drive away. Besides me, only Billy, your designer friend from your New York days, knew you were already married. Still married. That secret was our sword of Damocles. For months we had tried to make you unmarried, but B kept eluding you, stringing you along and then disappearing again, until here we were, a week away from the engraved date and no turning back—such is the power of a Crane's wedding invitation. I was very brave. I was very, very scared. At the marriage license bureau in Pittsburgh, I sat on a folding chair and stared at the pebbly pattern in the floor, waiting for our number to be called. It was 89, which felt auspicious, but still I felt I might be handcuffed and led away at any moment. I kept picturing my father's disappointment: *A bigamist?* As we walked down the aisle in the garden of my parents' house, two hulking duffel bags sat in the sunlit front hall holding the books you'd agreed to return to B to buy your freedom.

PIT – SFO | 1989

We were so poor—you a writer, me unsure what I was, both of us scraping by on book reviews and *Reader's*

Digest translations—it welded us together. Us against the world. Us alone in the world. Anxious but happy. Young and old at the same time. Our honeymoon was three nights only, more than we could afford. Breakfast each morning was an English muffin from the coffee shop across the street from our inn, and dinner was two take-out samosas from Burma House, which we placed on paper napkins on the bedspread between bites. We rode the bus—to Golden Gate Park, where we roamed under eucalyptus, to SFMOMA, where we watched Nicholas Nixon's wife and her sisters age under glass, to the Exploratorium, where we stood on a small platform and felt the earthquake of 1906, delighted as children.

CDG – PHL – PIT – PHL – CDG – PHL – PIT – PHL – CDG – PHL – PIT – CDG – PHL – PIT – CDG | 1989 1990 1991 1992 1993 1994 1995 1996 1997 1998

Four crossings a year, summer and Christmas. Always to see my parents. They paid for the tickets. Where else could we go? I never had the audacity to wonder. *DÉPARTS*: entubed escalators crossing in midair, lifting us up to the gates. Carton of Gitanes, bottle of Zubrowka in Duty Free. *ARRIVÉES*: it always felt too soon, somehow, to return to rent, uncertainty, and dog shit on sidewalks, our suitcases heavy with peanut butter and books. Woe to us if we landed alongside planes from PAP, DKR, ASK. The shapeless, swollen, shifting crowd creeping forward, the agents taking their time, stamping their colonialist disdain on the pages of the passports. The customs line was where the vacation feeling started to fade. Baggage claim was where it died.

CDG – PHL – PIT – LAX – PIT – CDG | 1991

A's wedding. This time we did leave my parents' house. We even left our son. Two nights. We landed and immediately felt out of place, a pair of woolly Woody Allens blinking and gauche in the dumb-blonde smile of the California sun. A fight in the rental car when you didn't read the map fast enough for me as I drove. Tears, indignant and powerless, when I learned our beloved A was to be bathed before the ceremony, as though she were unclean. *Barbaric*, you said. At the Beverly Wilshire Hotel she descended the stairs, her dark beautiful head floating above the white dress, seeming somehow separate from the rest of her. Deceased relatives were evoked. A wine glass was crushed under a heel. Chairs with people on them were hoisted in the air. We left in the night to return to our baby boy on the far coast, the coast we knew. As the plane rose, I looked out the window and the city was an overturned jewelry box, so much more beautiful than it was in daylight.

CDG – LHR | 1992

Sweet bright warm spring day. We went to the Food Halls at Harrods and blew our budget on two cups of coffee. Being poor here felt even poorer than being poor in Paris. That evening we attended the book party of one of our authors, T. (We had an imprint now, and though my name still did not appear, I found the books and you pushed them through to publication. My being your *éminence grise* seemed to suit us both.) The party was in an elegant row house in Kensington. A young woman in white chiffon was draped on a sofa and attended by other young women in white, looking like a mantelpiece by Saint-Gaudens. There were Renoirs on the walls and our clothes were all wrong. Besides T, we knew no one and wandered like unwanted stepchildren from walled garden to darkened parlor and back again. That evening was the first time I felt the weight of class pressing down from above—a distinct, atmospheric force. We didn't say this out loud. I think we didn't want to see each other diminished. You asked a spongy drunken aristocrat, *Do you know T's agent?* and he turned his head a notch, eyed you on the diagonal like a goshawk, and said, *My dear sir, I EMPLOY her.* As soon as we could, we took a black cab back to our borrowed flat and sang along to Monty Python's *Final Rip-off*, laughing until we cried.

ORY – CEQ | 1997

That lazy breezy blue atmosphere all hot-weather airports have—think STX, think SJM. We were going to C's wedding. The "first one," as it would later be known. It seemed impossible that we found ourselves in such a place. I swam in the Mediterranean. You floated on your back in the vast aquamarine pool, arms outstretched, "like Christ," you insisted on saying. That evening we sat at tables under palm trees in the warm twilight. I made a toast, quoted Shakespeare. The next morning, on the small television in our cool and beautiful room overlooking the sea, I wept as I watched Diana's boys follow her coffin through the wide streets of London. But mostly we were happy. We felt like people in a movie about people who vacation in such places. On the wedding day there were drinks on the rooftop, a ceremony by the pool, dancing into the night. On the way home, in the airport gift shop I bought a tablecloth with olives on it for your mother, to thank her for keeping our boy.

PVD | 1998 – 2015

This one became ours when we moved here in the last days of 1997. You stayed stubbornly nostalgic for the original: glass doors that did not open until you pushed them, a curving staircase that led to an observation deck, a tank filled with bubbling seawater where travelers could buy a lobster to take on the plane. You rejected the renovations that transformed it from a stucco Art Deco box to just one more late-20th century transit point, with its swooping roofline and glass curtain walls facing the runways. In the new terminal, there is a store called Explore!Rhode Island, where you can buy saltwater taffy and local maple syrup and wine from Sakonnet, and tubs of Del's Lemonade mix and Aristocrat coffee syrup. The one thing you do like about the new airport is the real sailboat on display on the ground floor. I wonder, will you ever come here again?

BOS – EWR – SAP | 2008

Fields of sugar cane as the plane came in for a landing. Ice cream and coffee stands in the cinder block terminal. Outside, the yellow light, the wall of heat. This one I landed in alone, when I found a place to do the work I craved. Wordless work. Work I could feel in my back, hands, legs, anywhere but in my head. Work that did not feel like "work," the stuff we office people try to do between meetings. Standing in the back of a pick-up truck, I rode south for two hours, out of the city and up and over and down the hills, to a town called Comayagua, where I spent days mixing cement and laying concrete blocks in heat that made my shins sweat. My fellow workers, these new colleagues, assumed that like them I was working for the glory of Christ. I kept quiet and leaned all my weight into the drill as I screwed sheets of corrugated metal to the roof beams. Life was sleep, eat, work, eat, sleep. I was scared by how happy I was. On the trip home, during an unplanned and complicated layover, I sat on the curb in a parking lot in Humble, Texas, and cried.

PVD – ORD | 2008

On the five-city jazz trip years earlier, stopping here between MSY and MCI, we met Charlie Parker's white trumpet player, Red Rodney, at the Blackstone Hotel; when we came this time, Millennium Park was being born in a construction site. After the book fair, we walked for miles, the enormity and heft of the city on our right, the ocean-like horizon on our left. In the marina (*A mar-*

ina on a lake! I kept saying, needing you to grasp the enormity of it) the sound of lines clanging against masts reminded me of waking up in an auberge in Trouville. That was before you. We wandered through an outdoor blues festival and then made our way to the Art Institute, where we peered through small rectangles of glass into ornate rooms the size of shoeboxes.

BOS – NAS – ASD | 2010

We wasted a night in NAS, unnerved by the booze cruises and the bland hotel food, but flights to the island were only every other day. Things had been hard for a long time. Novel after novel written, breath held. The reviews always positive, the sales never enough. We were tired, and winter was long. I wanted to surprise you: three days under the sun away from home. We played the slots in the casino. You bought Cuban cigars. The next day we walked onto the tarmac and boarded a small plane with no cockpit door. Over the pilot's shoulder we watched through the windshield as the loud little plane arced over absurdly turquoise water and came to rest at ASD. An old Bahamian in an '80s-model Ford station wagon drove us to a place of palm trees and conviviality. There were families, couples, chatty people on week-long vacations, and the scuba guides that are always in places like that— tan Germans and New Zealanders who act more easygoing than they are. By the time we got there we had only two nights and one day, which I spent reading your latest manuscript.

BOS – GVA – CDG | 2011

Layover: terminals like shining cities, the polyglot trains slipping sleekly under them. No e-cigs, hair extensions, or acne products. Instead, something in the air—an assumption that all who pass through here are people of vast means. Leather bags like architectural maquettes. Glass cases holding watches and chocolates. Illuminated jewelry ads as beautiful as the jewels themselves. The scalloped collars and white gloves of the saleswomen told me that this is where civility went when it disappeared from the rest of the world. The guilt of wanting to stay here in this gleaming neutral biosphere where I was nobody, when in fact I was on my way to help you bury your mother. Her coffin looked like it was built for a bird.

BOS – CDG | 2015

Terminal E, lower level, where all the French kids appeared when they came to visit over the years, walking shyly through the automatic doors, scanning the crowd, letting themselves be gathered up by us and escorted out into the night, the Prudential Tower standing tall against the sky—*Bienvenue aux Etats Unis!*—and taken home to the big old house in Providence. On the upper level, so many long, joking send-offs—the snaking line, the machines swallowing bags and shoes, the final waves and the disappearing. This is where you will come, but there will be no goodbye. The goodbye will already have happened, on a sidewalk. You will be alone. You will have a one-way ticket. And maybe our hearts will have broken.

And maybe our hearts will mend. And maybe you will know, as you are lifted up over the harbor and the unbearable sadness of flying moves through you, that everything is going to be all right. That the pain in your chest is not greater than the promise of whatever new thing you're moving toward, that the morning that is still six hours away might for once break not gray but bright and bracing, a challenge and an invitation you will be ready to accept.

i say this only with love
Emily Lake Hansen

Despite your grandmother's example, your thumb is not green. In Arizona, where you lived briefly after college, you even killed a small cactus. Your husband laughed when he noticed it on the mantel, shriveled and brown. *You killed a cactus in the desert!* he cackled. Its short limbs had begun to hollow. Where spikes had been, there were now just indentations, holes where defenses once stood. You let it sit decaying for a few weeks afterwards in its small blue pot. Eventually it looked so fragile that you thought about pushing it gently with your finger, wanted to know if it had become so hollow inside that a simple gesture might break it completely. When you finally touched it, the needles had softened so much they grazed against your fingers like silk.

Your newest therapist tells you one day as you are sitting on her couch, your arms wound up, crossed into a tight protective knot, that even if trauma has been intellectually processed, the body can hold on to it. What a racket, you think, and squeeze your legs tighter and tighter together. You wonder if maybe there are more muscles you can tighten in order to become smaller, to hide better beneath the mound of pillows on the couch. What would it take to become an ant, you wonder? To be so small you might be able to crawl into the lush fern at the corner of the room and remain unseen forever.

In the book *The Body Keeps the Score*—assigned to you as homework by your therapist, you've read it cover to cover now twice—the psychiatrist Bessel van der Kolk writes that trauma "is not just an event that took place sometime in the past; it is also the imprint left by that experience on mind, brain, and body. This imprint has ongoing consequences for how the human organism manages to survive in the present."

The thing you remember most about your grandmother—besides the time in the late stages of her life when you watched as a nurse poked a needle into the crux of her arm, drew from it vial after vial of blood—is her garden. On the large, covered porch of her house in Melbourne, Florida, not the last place she lived, but the second to last, the place you remember best, she maintained a magnificent garden. There was no dirt from which to really grow things, so she lined shelf after shelf full of potted plants instead: geraniums, multicolored petunias, hot pink zinnias—your favorite—even marigolds, a bright yellow like the sun, all nestled in terra cotta pots. She hung even more flowers along the trellis—chrysanthemums and touch-me-nots in short plastic planters strung up with thick twine. You can remember being handed the large green watering can, hoisting it up on your shoulder so you could sprinkle water over the plants, help them bloom.

As you get to know the new therapist, she pushes you harder. After you discuss a feeling or traumatic memory, she asks you to sit with it. *Sit with it?* you balk, crossing your arms again. You're used to placing your feelings into a locked tackle box as soon as they materialize, storing them right away alongside freeze-dried worms and shiny metal hooks, pushing them under the bed with the dust bunnies, with the bins of clothes you've outgrown since your pregnancy. *How do you sit with a feeling?* you have to ask. After all, you're just now beginning to name them, to print from the label maker in your brain tiny white stickers: sad, mad, scared, lonely. You're only given the most basic vocabulary to start with. You're like a child in a kindergarten classroom, the furniture and materials around you all labeled to help you learn to read: sink, book, backpack, jacket.

Van der Kolk writes, "Traumatized people chronically feel unsafe inside their bodies: the past is alive in the form of gnawing interior discomfort. Their bodies are constantly bombarded by visceral warning signs, and, in an attempt to control these processes, they often become expert at ignoring their gut feelings and in numbing awareness of what is played out inside."

Your mother is neither as gifted as her mother nor as inept as you at tending a garden. When she moves out of your last childhood home, she takes with her one potted plant: a red winged begonia known for being tough. Drought-resistant, the begonia is also self-cleaning—it drops flowers on its own as they die. Your mother is proud of the plant's resilience, brings it inside just in case though under each threat of frost. She is happy to report that she has managed to keep some portion of the plant alive for nearly 15 years by clipping off pieces and replanting them. In the most recent iteration, the begonia has begun to overgrow its host pot. She knows she'll need to clip more soon to keep it alive, won't hesitate to make the cut.

When invited to housewarmings, she often gives a clipping in a carefully selected ceramic pot to the new homeowner. When you buy your first home, she gets you a trash can instead, a tall, cream colored one that takes bags you have to special order off the internet. *You would have killed the plant*, she tells you directly as you open the large rectangular box that contains the trash bin.

When you tell the therapist you're anxious, she doesn't take it at its face value. Instead, she demands that you survey your body from top to bottom to identify the places where it hurts. *Where in your body is the anxiety?* she asks you, as if your body is a separate being entirely from the mind you use to control it.

You try earnestly because you don't like being a disappointment. *There's a crunching in the thighs*, you say, *a numbness in the stomach, almost like hunger, a tension running through the shoulders.*

Good, she says, as if you've answered a difficult question, *that's good.* She asks you to breathe into each of those places, to picture your breath like a light you could shine on each spot where it hurts. The very act of calling attention to the pain is supposed to relieve it. Van der Kolk writes that traumatized individuals often "learn to hide from their selves."

The year you were seven your father was out to sea on the USS Lincoln, his second deployment since your birth, and your grandmother visited you and your mother for over a month. Over the course of her visit, she enlisted your help to plant a garden on the small plot of land behind the apartment that belonged to your parents as tenants. With her, you kneeled in the silty California soil, dug up holes so you could plant stalks of sunflowers, bulbs of tulips. Your mother stood at the sliding glass door and snapped a picture: in it, you are wearing oversized gardening gloves, your hands deep in the dirt. Your grandmother is perched behind you, holding a small shovel. She is not looking at the camera, you notice one day, thumbing the copy of the photograph that sits on your dresser, but rather directly at you.

Although you've told your new therapist about the bad days, the cloudy ones where it's hard to pull yourself from your bed, where you want to collapse on her office couch as soon as you walk into the room, you haven't actually laid down on the couch ever. Once, bravely, you tucked your knees up under your legs, leaned a bit on the cushion.

But even then, from the semi-relaxed position, you felt exposed, as if in relaxing your body, you might be letting the therapist too far into your mind as well. You know this is the space for the ugly bits, for the parts you're too afraid to look at alone in the mirror, but you still have boundaries, iron gates overgrown with ivy.

Van der Kolk writes that "as long as you keep secrets and suppress information, you are fundamentally at war with yourself. The critical issue is allowing yourself to know what you know. That takes an enormous amount of courage."

At the next duty station where you lived from ages eight to ten, your mother didn't keep as many plants and your grandmother was too sick to visit. Instead, your mother let things stay mostly wild in the small, fenced backyard: desert soil and yarrow, citrus trees blooming fruit at the top of the steep hill. From the edge of the fence, the valley below seemed to descend infinitely into a pit of tickytack houses, a ditch filled with red Spanish tile and desert shrubs. You were in that backyard when you got news of your grandmother's death. Your mother, who had spent the last month in Florida, taking turns with her siblings at your grandmother's bedside, had called your father from the hospital and told him that it had finally happened. Your father then passed the news along to you. *Okay*, you had sighed, staring down into the valley, what else was there to say?

It's from the memories of that house too—you remember watching the small lemons drop from the corner tree, you remember walking from the patio through the French doors into your parents' bedroom, remember tracing your hands along the green walls in the hallway, remember turning the corner into the dining room, remember taking the three shallow steps down into the sunken den, remember sitting down on the tan striped couch, its raised furry lines cutting indentations into your legs—that you uncover as if from underneath a thick sheet of soil: the time your mother French kissed you.

I thought you wanted to know what it was like, she told you as you backed away from her on the striped couch. *It's not a big deal, jeez. You acted like you wanted it.*

Okay, you said and stood up, retreated slowly down the long hallway to your room. What else was there to do?

When you arrive at that particular memory with the new therapist, you spend less time filling in the details of the occurrence and more time defending your mother. Your limbs are twisted so tightly that you are afraid your muscles might tear from their connective tissue in stress. *She isn't so much a predator,* you try to explain, *as someone without boundaries. She often treated me like a friend. I was just learning about puberty and kissing.* She thought it would help. Or maybe you really did ask for it, you think. You are the turning mechanism of a wind-up music box, twisted and twisted clockwise until you can no longer budge; soon you will have no choice but to spin the other way and from you, music will spill into the air like a dense and sudden fog.

Van der Kolk writes, "The essence of trauma is that

it is overwhelming, unbelievable, and un-bearable. Each patient demands that we suspend our sense of what is normal and accept that we are dealing with a dual reality: the reality of a relatively secure and predictable present that lives side by side with a ruinous, ever-present past."

Your grandmother had been dead for four years by the time your mother attempted a death stunt of her own. In the bathroom attached to your bedroom, the door locked with a flimsy hook and eye latch, she went for a swim in the old narrow bathtub after swallowing a handful of pills. The next morning when your father sat you down in the kitchen and tried to explain what had happened, the doctors were still unsure of the exact type of pill she had taken and could tell your father only that they had to pump her stomach, weren't sure for a minute if she would live.

In your fourteen-year-old mind, unable to process what you'd been told, you imagined your mother as one of the mermaids she admired, a lady at the Weeki Wachee theme park with a fake blue tail, fingering strands of seaweed as she twirled under the water.

When you're unsure of the feeling word to fill in the blank with (*You felt —— when your mother attempted suicide, you felt —— when your father pierced his belly button at 40, you feel —— when you picture now your father's car pulling away from your mother's new apartment*), your therapist makes you sit silently. *It will come*, she promises, though you are often convinced it's a lie akin to advertisement, a wish instead of a prediction. Sometimes instead of reaching for the feeling word, you count the stems on the office fern: one branch, two branches, three branches, four. In a pinch, you simply say you feel numb, which your therapist will accept sometimes. Other times, when she can tell that you're lying, she will insist on you trying again. *I'll close my eyes if you want,* she tells you. She knows you don't like to be looked at.

Van der Kolk writes, "Beneath the surface of the protective parts of trauma survivors there exists an undamaged essence, a Self that is confident, curious, and calm, a Self that has been sheltered from destruction by the various protectors that have emerged in their efforts to ensure survival. Once those protectors trust that it is safe to separate, the Self will spontaneously emerge, and the parts can be enlisted in the healing process."

Your grandmother, you're told, was the first person to hold you. After your birth at the Naval hospital in Portsmouth, Virginia, the doctors handed you, freshly swaddled and rinsed of the aftermath of birth, not to your mother, but to your grandmother. She held you for whole minutes in her arms before she handed you back to a nurse, rushed downstairs to the hospital gift shop to buy a bouquet of flowers for your mother's room: yellow roses and baby's breath in a pink cellophane wrapper.

You don't remember that moment, obviously, but your mother points to it sometimes to explain your connection to your grandmother, to explain why you always seemed to like her better. Even on her deathbed, your mother says one day, *you were her favorite, that portrait of you as a toddler, your hair still golden and curly, in a silver frame next to her hospital bed.*

You don't mean to cry when you tell your therapist about your grandmother—such an old wound, you think, remembering that she has been dead for two thirds of your life by this point — but you do cry a little upon reopening your eyes, a surprise wetness trickling down your cheeks. You wonder if you might water the fern with it, wet the leaves with your tears, be useful. Your therapist asks you where it hurts and you figure the correct answer is everywhere, but you say aloud instead, *my head feels heavy, my feet a little numb.*

Van der Kolk writes, "Children are also programmed to choose one particular adult (or at most a few) with whom their natural communication system develops. This creates a primary attachment bond. The more responsive the adult is to the child, the deeper the attachment and the more likely the child will develop healthy ways of responding to the people around him."

Your mother's relationship with her mother, your grandmother, is by all accounts much different than your own. These are the stories you are told: your grandmother was in her 40s by the time she had your mother and so was already exasperated with parenting, she often left your mother to her own devices for days on end, which resulted in adventures such as regularly swimming in a rainwater filled ditch, getting sun poisoning once on a beach vacation, and being raped by a high school teacher she had naively befriended. Your grandmother, also as a consequence of being so removed from parenting, repeatedly ignored the signs that your aunt, nineteen years older than your mother, was physically abusive when left in charge. Your grandmother, despite knowing how to sew, cook well enough, and garden exquisitely, did not teach these skills to your mother. Your grandmother, one time while riding on a bus, gave away your mother's all-day sucker to stop another kid from crying.

The scariest thing you say aloud to your therapist is this: *I don't know if I really love my mother* by which you actually mean you don't love her the way you're supposed to. Even thinking it makes you feel like a monster. From your perch at the edge of the couch, you squeeze your body tightly as if you're in the middle seat of an airplane, worried your limbs, the meat of your thighs, will cross immediately into your neighbor's space if you relax.

And how does that make you feel? your therapist asks predictably. By now you're used to the game, the give and take you step into once you cross the threshold of her office.

Guilty, you respond, an easy answer, but you know the real answer is sad even though you've taught yourself it's pointless to feel sad about the things you can't control. Van der Kolk writes, "Parental abuse is not the only cause of disorganized attachment: Parents who are preoccupied with their own trauma, such as domestic abuse or rape or the recent death of a parent or sibling, may also be too emotionally unstable and inconsistent to offer much comfort and protection. While all parents need all the help they can get to raise secure children, traumatized parents, in particular, need help to be attuned to their children's needs."

At the house you buy with your husband, you leave the yard work, the mowing, the gardening mostly to him. You try for a while to be helpful, trim the English ivy that lines your front walk, do some raking in the fall, but eventually you both decide that it's easier to let the yard get a little wild. Clover sprouts fluffy white heads in the summer, your camellias grow tall like trees, sometimes wild strawberries even bloom, small red hearts nestled among weeds.

 Once a month your husband spends the weekend in the yard, cutting down what he must so there's space for your children to roam, for the dog to do its business. You watch him from the kitchen window, peering over the line of knickknacks you've placed there over the years. Among the keepsakes—tiny art prints, empty wine bottles—are three now dead plants, given to you as gifts on different occasions: as a thank you for serving as room parent, as a wedding favor, as a mother's day present from your older son, a small now decayed fern in a haphazardly painted pot splashed with aquamarine glitter.

A few months into therapy, trying to work, at your therapist's insistence, on not overthinking how much space you take up in the world, you make a joke on Instagram about not being able to keep plants alive. *Except that part about loving plants,* you write on a repost of a story about Virgos, *I kill cacti in the desert* 😂 😂

Your husband's cousin replies to your post almost instantly: *not being able to care for plants is a reflection of not caring enough for the self. i say this only with love.*

Van der Kolk writes, "As we grow up, we gradually learn to take care of ourselves, both physically and emotionally, but we get our first lessons in self-care from the way that we are cared for. Mastering the skill of self-regulation depends to a large degree on how harmonious our early interactions with our caregivers are."

After the suicide attempt, your aunt, your mother's middle sister, took you to the psychiatric ward of Baptist Hospital so you could visit your mother. It's not that you wanted to see your mother at all, just that it was the right thing to do, your aunt told you, and so you climbed into her green Subaru and rode reluctantly across town to the hospital. On the way, your aunt stopped at a grocery store to pick out flowers, asked you to be the one to give the small bouquet of white and yellow daisies to your mother—you reached out cautiously to hand her the flowers when you arrived, it was the first time you had seen her since her swim in the bathtub.

During the visit, your mother showed you and your aunt around the building, took you on a tour of her small room, introduced you to the other crazies (her words, not yours), walked you into the main sitting area where an elaborate arts and crafts table sat in the far corner. *That's where I spend most of my time*, your mother said, babbling on about the limited things she could do there, about how they weren't allowed scissors or staplers, how even pipe cleaners were forbidden, so instead they made bracelets out of rubber bands and small plastic beads, the kind meant for children.

Until it broke when you were 27, you kept the small rubber band bracelet on your nightstand. Eventually the rubber wore down so much where it had been tied that its bond disintegrated, and the beads fell to the floor like loud, loose marbles.

One day you tell your therapist a story about a recent visit to your mother's: *I called her out about something, you start, I pushed where I shouldn't have, I was in the middle of trying to cook dinner for everyone, I said something like go ahead and walk away, blame me, you did it my whole childhood. And she got so mad, you could just see it on her face. And she was like my god, I don't know what I did. You're still walking around holding these grudges. All we can do is do better than our parents. I did and you are too.*

You take a deep breath when you've finished the story, try to shine a spotlight, just like your therapist has told you to, onto all the places that hurt. But for the first time, you know it's really everything and nothing that hurts all at once. You think maybe, for all her faults, your mother got that one thing right: we're all just trying to do better than our parents. You imagine the tall begonia sitting on your mother's new back porch, its red wings visible through the doors she replaced last summer with glass. There's no use in hating her. She's learned at least, you think, picturing the tiny buckets of begonia clippings sitting in neat stacks, to take care of herself.

After a few more months of therapy, you begin to wonder if the fern in the therapist's office is real. Each time you see it, it seems impossibly green, lush and full as if the office is some climate-controlled greenhouse with an expert gardener on hand each day to trim away the dead parts and water what's still growing *just the right* amount. One day as you leave the office, you run a finger along a stem, brush your hand against a particularly green leaf—you know now: real.

Contributors

Lorelei Bacht's poetic work has appeared/ is forthcoming in *The Night Heron Barks, Queerlings, SoFloPoJo, Barrelhouse, Sinking City, Stoneboat, One Art, SWWIM*, and elsewhere. They can be found on Twitter @bachtlorelei and on Instagram @lorelei.bacht.writer. They are currently watching the rain instead of working on a chapbook.

Anon Baisch is currently a data analyst working in the semiconductor industry. Anon's poems have been published most recently in *Defunct, New Note Poetry, 2River, The Write Launch*, and forthcoming in *Waxing & Waning*.

Dalanie Beach is a nonbinary creative writer and visual artist from Anderson, IN. Their work has appeared in *East Fork Journal of the Arts* and is forthcoming in *Drunk Monkeys* and *Glassworks*. They hold an MFA in Creative Writing from Miami University (OH) and are currently working on their PhD in Fiction at Ohio University.

Brett Biebel teaches writing and literature at Augustana College in Rock Island, IL. His (mostly very) short fiction has appeared in *Hobart, SmokeLong Quarterly, The Masters Review, Wigleaf*, and elsewhere. It's also been chosen for Best Small Fictions and as part of Wigleaf's annual Top 50 Very Short Stories. *48 Blitz*, his debut story collection, is available from Split/Lip Press.

Emily Bilman, PhD writes in Geneva, CH. Her dissertation, *The Psychodynamics of Poetry* was published by Lambert Academic in 2010 and *Modern Ekphrasis* by Peter Lang in 2013. Her poetry books, *A Woman by A Well* (2015), *Resilience* (2015), *The Threshold of Broken Waters* (2018) and *Apperception* (2020) were all published by Troubador, UK. She blogs on http://www.emiliebilman.wix.com/emily-bilman

Rohan Buettel lives in Canberra, Australia. His haiku have appeared in various Australian and international journals (including *Frogpond, Cattails* and *The Heron's Nest*). His longer poetry recently appears in *The Elevation Review, Rappahannock Review, Penumbra Literary and Art Journal, Mortal Magazine, Passengers Journal, Reed Magazine, Meniscus,* and *Quadrant.*

Sarah Dayley (she/they) is a writer and artist from Oakland, California, unceded Muwekma Ohlone territory. Sarah is a Hambidge Fellow whose work can be found in *Duende*, the *Berkeley Poetry Review*, the *West Trade Review*, and on sarahdayley.com.

Laine Derr holds an MFA from Northern Arizona University and has published interviews with Carl Phillips, Ross Gay, Ted Kooser, and Robert Pinsky. Recent work has appeared or is forthcoming from *Antithesis, ZYZZYVA, Portland Review, North Dakota Quarterly, Prairie Schooner,* and elsewhere.

Nanami Fetter lives in Portland, Oregon. Her works have

been featured in *The Magazine*, *Pathos Literary Magazine*, *Sapling*, and *Drunk Monkeys*.

Isabella Garces is a Colombian writer based in Brooklyn, New York. She produces content for The Metropolitan Museum of Art and her writing can be found in *Esquire*, *Popshot Magazine*, and *la piccioletta barca*, among others.

Robin Gow is a trans and queer poet and YA/MG author from rural Pennsylvania. They are the author of several poetry collections, an essay collection, and a YA novel in verse, *A Million Quiet Revolutions*.

Former athlete and relapsed student, **Kolena Jones Kayembe** is a Caribbean-Canadian writer, editor, and photographer. Forever on the move—from the Americas to Europe, Asia, Middle East and Africa—she is currently based in Paris, France, where she reads too much about existentialism and tries to find a sustainable work/life balance in an increasingly remote and fast-changing world. Her writing and photography have appeared in *The Meadow* (forthcoming), *The/tEmz/Review*, *Spellbinder Magazine*, *Typishly*, *Kunstraum Retz*, and *Art Forum*.

Max Kruger-Dull holds an MFA in Writing from Vermont College of Fine Arts. His recent work has appeared or is forthcoming in *The MacGuffin*, *Litro Magazine*, *Hunger Mountain Review*, *the tiny journal*, *The Broadkill Review*, and others. He lives in New York with his boyfriend and two dogs.

Emily Lake Hansen (she/her) is a fat, bisexual poet and memoirist and the author of *Home and Other Duty Stations* (Kelsay Books). Her work has appeared in *32 Poems*, *The McNeese Review*, *The Shore*, and *So to Speak* among others. She lives in Atlanta where she teaches at Agnes Scott College.

Lucian McDowell's work has appeared in *Salon*, *The Rumpus*, *The Lindenwood Review*, *Thread/Stitch*, the *Christian Science Monitor*, and elsewhere, as well as in numerous university magazines.

Mary Elise Myers recently moved to Albuquerque, New Mexico from New England and teachers High School English and History in this desert city. She has lived in many places including, Boston, Cork, Ireland, Beer Sheva, Israel and Catalonia, Spain. She is a feminist and advocates for students who identify as LBGTQ+ as well as honoring neurodivergence in her learning community. She has a daughter, partner, and enormous Maine Coon cat. The author has been recently published in *Tofu Ink* and *Logic 86*. She marvels at the wonders and magic of "the Land of Enchantment" and has learned how to eat green and red chili three times a day.

Heidi Nieling is a fiber artist living in southern Minnesota with her husband and two six-year-olds. Her flash CNF, "Chicken Legs," was recently published in *Vast Chasm Magazine*, and she will have two pieces published in *Ruby* in October, 2022. Heidi can be found on Instagram @heidi_nieling

Cassady O'Reilly-Hahn is a poet with an MA from Claremont Graduate University. He is a managing editor for *Foothill: A Poetry Journal* and a Scripting Editor at Deluxe, a company that localizes TV and Film. Cassady writes Haiku for his Instagram @cassady_orha. He currently resides in Redlands, California.

Marina Ramil is a lifelong reader and writer whose work has been featured in the *Stoneboat Literary Journal* and elsewhere. They live in South Florida (for now) with kid sisters, alligators, and strangler figs. They can be found on Twitter and Instagram @thesuncomingout.

Melissa Rotert is a University of Buffalo graduate who writes speculative fiction for all ages. Her short works attempt to capture the whimsy of her full length kidlit. Born in the Midwest and raised in WNY, Melissa is a theatre geek turned writer with work published in *INKbabies* literary magazine.

Sabin Timalsena is an algorithmic artist who describes his work as computational poetry—writing in the language of machines to create art for humans. He makes art with mathematics and code, exploring natural systems and the emergence of complexity from simple rules and vice versa. He strives to push the boundaries of what's possible in algorithmic art and is constantly in the process of establishing/enhancing a vocabulary of algorithms that allow him to express himself through original computer programs. Sometimes he uses algorithms as a brush, and sometimes he gives the brush to the algorithms. "Meshing of Dreams," the cover art for this anthology, is based on the observation that oftentimes there is continuity between dreams, where some events, objects, and memories from one dream are also present in the next. One dream can seed another, and one person's dream can instigate another's dream. Made with code (C++/openFrameworks)

Made in United States
Orlando, FL
03 March 2023